Standing on the Word of God

Dr. Daniel Kazemian

NEW HARBOR PRESS

RAPID CITY, SD

Kazemian/New Harbor Press
1601 Mt. Rushmore Rd, Ste 3288
Rapid City, SD 57701
www.NewHarborPress.com

Ordering Information:
Quantity sales. Special discounts are available on quantity purchases by corporations, associations, and others. For details, contact the "Special Sales Department" at the address above.

Standing on the Word of God / Dr. Daniel Kazemian -- 1st ed.
ISBN 978-1-63357-251-5

Contents

Introduction

In this book, we will be learning how we can stand on the Word of God. We live by faith and believing God that He will never fail us.

Reading, declaring, meditating, and establishing our hearts on His word. By the Spirit of Living God, and He will allow us to grow in a new life.

He will reveal His promise through our daily living when we speak **'Life'** into our situations.

We experience there is no doubt and not speaking negatives to our circumstances, these wrong speak cannot be useful.

In this book, we will learn how to speak the right word by faith. Declaring the Word in our prayer for receiving the answer will take place from the Lord.

We don't need to use these words: **"'I hope' the Lord will answer my prayer or heal me."** Another word we use: **"If 'it's God's will,' He will heal me"**

These words are not working in the Kingdom of God. Every Word and every promise of God is: **Yes, and Amen.** It is already done. Praise the Lord.

His word is a lamp to our feet and a light to our path. The Holy Spirit is working in every aspect of every person's life to bring them into a knowledge of the Son of God.

The affirmation of God is to bring life and prosperity to us. We continue standing on God's Word, He will never ever fail anyone.

He will manifest His power and love through healing, miracles, blessings to us every day.

I will be using my personal experience, many scriptures, and stories from the Bible. Then, we can learn by opening our hearts and getting inspired by the Word?

We will be studying and growing in the spirit and building up a good foundation for our faith.

Discovering God's plan, which we built our lives on God's Word. We are standing on the promise and the guidance of the Spirit.

As, we review all-powerful stories with brief records in the Bible.

I believe every part of the Word of God; every story can teach us and lead us into our destiny in life.

CHAPTER 1

The Word of God

The Word is God and is with God. Therefore, we are receiving the Word by faith. His word brings revelation, salvation, knowledge, wisdom to our lives.

Why do we, as Christians, accept the Bible, because the Word is the powerful spiritual Law by God?

We recognize God's magnificent performance in all His achievements, which is declaring to perfection.

"In the beginning was the Word, and the Word was with God, and the Word was God." John 1:1, NKJV.

We believe in Jesus by faith; we have fruits of the spirit. The world will know us who we are in Christ.

We profoundly wish that everyone will explore for themselves the revelation of God Almighty.

The Word Revealed to Us:

"The Word" has been revealed by the Spirit of God in unique ways.

God has declared His Word to the entire world to make a relationship by giving His love to His people.

His Word is well carried out by the specific time and by His chosen person to reach out to His people.

The Lord God has appointed all His servants; prophets, chosen Kings, and Apostles.

God has chosen those servants to write God's Word by inspiration of His Spirit. It can likewise be called **"the Word of God."**

We believe the Word is written by the revelation of the Spirit of **God** without error at the beginning of writings. The spoken Word is His Voice by God Himself.

The Word has divine authority and supreme power. It has absolute law to execute judgment in teaching, correction, and discipline.

God Cannot Lie:

We believe in the truthfulness of God through His Word. Then He reveals Himself to us in many ways.

God has used many forms of choosing His people who were willing to write God's words. **The Author of the Bible is God.**

We believe the Bible is the unchangeable, uncheckable, immutable Living Word of God.

This is especially accurate because the Bible states that God cannot lie. We should read His Word as we study and learn His plan.

As we recognize, the Holy Spirit testifies to the accuracy of scripture. God has recorded all His books in the form of the Bible.

Apply The Word:

We need to look at these three elements to apply the Word for ourselves.

1. **Reading and studying the Word.**
2. **Believing in our hearts and understanding the Word.**

3. **Practicing and experiencing the Word of God.**

We must meditate on God's Word will benefit us to get mature in faith. Only the Word will help us to become in **Christ-likeness.**

So, we may develop our spiritual lives on the truthfulness of God. We should learn God's Word.

Most remarkable of all, **He, Himself, dwells in the Word.** The Bible is an extraordinary record of history and laws.

It would confirm that there is a God that made all things. His will and His plan for every one of our lives.

That is why God gave His Word to obey Him to walk righteously before His presence.

God's Word Takes us to the Truth:

Although many of us grew in the Lord by learning by ourselves about God.

But when we take the Word into our hearts for knowing the way of salvation by ourselves.

It prepares us strongly, clearly by the revelation of the Spirit of God by simply knowing the Bible.

We are believing in the accuracy of Scripture. If we take the Lord's directions to heart.

He will reveal to us where to move, what to do, and how to act for any decision.

His Word also tells when we're making a wrong direction in life. He warns us of the resolves of a dangerous way of life.

Jesus as the living Word:

As we know, the Bible describes Jesus as the living Word. We experience the Bible is full of a collection of Words.

No errors can be found and even we cannot remove any Word out of the Bible.

Every Word is coming out of the mouth of God shall be established.

All scriptures in the Bible are precisely directed from our Almighty God, in which every Word is an Eternal message for us.

"So shall My word be that goes forth from My mouth;

It shall not return to Me void,

But it shall accomplish what I please,

And it shall prosper *in the thing* **for which I sent it."** Isaiah 55:11, NKJV.

Because He lives forever, He has authority over His Words and rules our lives.

The Bible has rich messages for all humankind and has a powerful effect on every life.

If we take in all His knowledge into our hearts and receive them. We will live with abounding blessings. The Word will teach us to grow like Jesus.

The Bible Statement:

As we know, the Bible reveals an existence and a living being of the Almighty God. The Word of God reveals who God is.

It is one of the most fundamental elements for experiencing and fellowship with God. We're encouraged to learn the Word to understand God.

The statement about **"the Word of God"** is higher than the human words.

God is a Living Spirit and has been talking into the human being since the beginning of formation.

He communicates with us and reveals His Glory to us throughout history. Through His creation, His prophets, His Scripture, His Son Jesus, and the Holy Spirit.

We can understand His messages to know God by pursuing Him and to discover Him in every situation.

Living Word:

It described that Jesus is divine as the Word, Life, and Light. It tells us about the Word, Jesus, who created and formed all things.

Life of Jesus Himself entered the world and lived among people.

The significance of calling Jesus is the Word in these verses represents the appearances of Jesus as both divine and human.

Throughout the Gospel of John are generally mentioned, confirming Jesus as the Son of God, **the eternal "Word"** who also lived on earth.

The Bible is a living message of love from the Father given to the lost world.

The Living God is alive from the beginning, and He works in this world through His living Word. The Holy Spirit is given to the Body of Christ as a gift to the church.

The doctrine of Christian faith is established on the **Living Word of God.**

It is fundamental in God's sovereignty as operates in creation, formation, authority, and salvation.

"And the Word became flesh and dwelt among us, and we beheld His glory, the glory as of the only begotten of the Father, full of grace and truth." John 1:14, NKJV.

The True Word:

The Word is truth, we must respond to God's Word by **Faith!** Believing that God is Spirit, **His Word is Life for our spirit, soul, and body.**

We must believe it because it is perfect, accurate, and truthful. We read it; we should seek to obey Him. This is the pure way to please God by faith.

The Word is spiritual bread for the spirit, soul. Our bodies needed healing by declaring His Word.

Our minds become refreshed by His Word for a Christian believer. Those who have entered the Kingdom of God by faith and must be born-again in Christ.

That's why it's important to learn, study, and meditate on it. We must saturate our minds with the

Scripture. The Word is fullness of life will cover our minds to protect us.

"All Scripture is given by inspiration of God, and is profitable for doctrine, for reproof, for correction, for instruction in righteousness." 2 Timothy 3:16, NKJV.

66 Books in the Bible:

Let's have a review about how many books are in the Bible. There are indicated in the Bible consists of **66 books** with two separate parts.

As we studied, the Old Testament consists of **39 books**, and the New Testament has **27 books.**

We discover in the book of Isaiah is pointed out about the birth of Jesus in the Old Testament.

"For unto us, a Child is born,

Unto us a Son is given;

And the government will be upon His shoulder.

And His name will be called,

Wonderful, Counselor, Mighty God,

Everlasting Father, Prince of Peace." Isaiah 9:6, NKJV.

We see the Word has declared approximately 800 years ago before by Prophet Isaiah has prophesied about Jesus' physical birth.

The prophetic word has been fulfilled by revelations of God which the Messiah should come to save the world.

His death and His resurrection for the whole world will have occurred in New Testament.

There is great evidence of Jesus' life, ministry in the Four Gospels, **Matthew, Mark, Luke, and John.**

Trinity:

We believe in Jesus by faith; we have fruits of the spirit. The world will know us who we are in Christ.

We profoundly wish that everyone will explore for themselves the revelation of God Almighty.

As we believe the Trinity, God is One in three persons:

- **God the Father as the Creator**
- **God the Son as the Savior**
- **God the Holy Spirit as Teacher, Comforter, and Guider.**

We don't need to allow any man would have the authority over God's Word. We must recognize God's Word can rule over us.

We learn to honor God's Word, build up our spirit to respect His sovereignty. We are living fearfully by the law of God.

We establish all families in the faith of Christ and our personal convictions for true biblical doctrine.

He is able to change us into a new man and woman of God by His power. Amen.

Truthful Word:

God is perfectly truthful, and the Bible is the inspired word of God. Therefore, it can be based on experiencing the Bible; it is true and the authoritative Word of God.

The Bible brings spiritual revelation to God's people. It teaches us to have a desire to experience His Glory.

To live in peace with each other and have intimacy with their Creator. God has chosen various ways of revealing himself to mankind

Every person would have a desire for an intimate relationship with each other. It's also important to remember that He will reveal Himself to us by the Holy Spirit.

People must have genuine and accurate evidence of their beliefs. We must establish our faith in the Word of God.

The Bible is a historical fact in perfect holiness and righteousness. Proof comes from the spiritual and physical manifestation of a Creator.

It brings glorious tangible of God's presence and glory. He reveals the expression of His love with a new relationship in our lives.

"The entirety of Your word is truth,

And every one of Your righteous judgments endures forever." Psalm 119:160, NKJV.

Holy Word:

The Word of God is Living and Powerful. The messages in the Bible have God's holy Words with power and with living life in them. As we discover in the coming verses.

The Word of God will protect us from sin when we examine ourselves. To allow us to meditate on the Word, day and night.

To understand a manifestation of the Word, and when we ask the Lord anything in prayer. He will speed up to answer our petition.

The secret of worship is to love Him and adore Him. We must acknowledge Him in a bad or good time because He loves us very much.

Keeping our love for God in our spirit and controlling our thoughts and actions.

Cleaning our hearts by the Word of God, constantly renewing our minds daily.

"For the word of God is living and powerful, and sharper than any two-edged sword, piercing even to the division of soul and spirit, and of joints and marrow, and is a discerner of the thoughts and intents of the heart." Hebrews 4:12, NKJV.

"Rhema":

Rhema is a Greek word referred for "Word." It relates to the actual spoken Words of God. The word **"Rhema"** means **"the spoken Word."**

The God-breathed spirit with the Living Word. He spoke with His power, His authority, and His sovereignty.

We usually need to understand between a divine and pure knowledge of God's Word. We must remember every Word is coming out of **the mouth of God is Life.**

Let's read about when Jesus was tempted by Satan, He answered.

"But He answered and said, "It is written, 'Man shall not live by bread alone, but by every word that proceeds from the mouth of God.'" Matthew 4:4, NKJV.

Logos:

The Word is the Lord Jesus. The term described as **"Word"** is logos, we can understand it as the absolute message of God to humanity.

The Word is alive and active to bring healing and life. Jesus showed the entire message, and that is why He is called the **"Logos" or "Word" of God.**

"Now the apostles and brethren who were in Judea heard that the Gentiles had also received the word of God." Acts 11:1, NKJV.

Scriptural Authority:

What is scriptural authority? The term theological doctrines refer to the attribute of God. It would make statements within the Old and New Testaments.

Theology means: the study of God and experiencing His triune personality. These biblical truths are authoritative over man's faith must live according to the Law of God.

There is the divine power to strengthen every believer who is in Christ. We submit ourselves under the Biblical truth.

Therefore, the context of history will inform the existence of God, and man can endure under the rule of God.

The Old Testament reveals with a demonstration of the creation of the world.

This particular story illustrates how the Almighty God is Creator who formed the world as a home for humankind.

When all creations have been completed successfully, then God created man in His own image.

From this powerful action, which God made it possible to glorify His Son, Jesus.

We see the Authority of God has manifested before and after creation. The evidence of God's existence continues for thousands of generations.

Although, until it goes on to the conclusion of the Old Testament in the times of Malachi. Christianity is established on a solid foundation of Christ.

We, as Christians, will recognize Jesus that He has full authority over the Church.

Because they know Him who came down from heaven as Son of God in human form.

Life Foundation:

The Word is establishing us on solid ground. The Bible is a strong life foundation for Christians and the church.

It will never tremble; however, it becomes the authority to transform our hearts from the inside out.

Let's ask ourselves or any believer about the power of God's Word. We would declare that the Word brings new life and turns into an abounding of joy.

God chooses to have a warm relationship with us, and despite seeing that we are not worthy, but He loves us. The Word will establish a love relationship between the Father and us.

When we read and meditate His Word to have contact with God through scriptures. We discover God's genuine love for us.

There is nothing else that matter and our hunger for Him better other things in the world. Nothing compares to having a close relationship with the Word of God.

His Word Leads Us:

God promises to lead us through every situation in our lives. He formed us with a special purpose and has a future for us.

We can identify the promise of His leadership over every life. He will be our shepherd indeed to the end.

While the Bible describes we will get His direction in life. How wonderful can be that we will receive them by faith to glorify His majestic name?

The Lord wants us to have a warm relationship with the Word. To experience Him through His Living Word.

This involves us spending time in His presence and meditating on His promise. God's commitment is to be our guider to bless us, and we praise His name. Amen.

Jesus, the Word:

When we believe in God's Word and the authority of His name. We are restored and delivered from all sins.

Faith in the Word makes us strong and sustains us in our belief that **Jesus is the Word**.

God's Word tells us that Jesus came to die on the cross for the sin of the world. God raised Him from the dead again for our salvation.

Let's look at the Word said about Jesus; **He pre-existed with God. He was with God. He is God.**

Jesus is the visible form of God's spirit. **"The Word,"** was the most perfect to characterize Jesus.

Although Jesus experienced His living on the earth as a man for a short time. He never rejected to do the plan of His Father.

He was revealing a message of Salvation of God with the fullness of Grace.

He is the Creator and all things have been created by Him and for Him. There would be nothing apart from Him. Amen.

Relationship with the Word:

The relationship with the Word is very significant, more than anything else.

Having a powerful desire for the Word would develop into a very vital part of spiritual growth.

The Holy Spirit will bring understanding to us; we spend time in His presence. Then we receive the fulness of His love toward us.

We will experience His Word by speaking and preaching His promise to ourselves.

Basically, the meaning of the Word signifies in the Bible: revealing God's power in creation.

The Names of God in Hebrew:

We learn many names of God in the Hebrew language in the Bible:

- **Jehovah-Elohim,** (The Eternal Creator) - Genesis 1:1
- **Adonai,** (God is Lord) - Malachi 1:6
- **Jehovah,** (God is I AM) - Genesis 2:4
- **El-Elion,** (The Lord Most High) - Isaiah 14:13-14
- **El-Shaddai,** (All-Sufficient One for the needs of His people) - Psalm 91:1

- **Jehovah-Jireh,** (The Lord our Provider) - Genesis 22:13-14

- **Jehovah-Nissi,** (The Lord our Banner) - Exodus 17:15

- **Jehovah-Rapha,** (The Lord our Healer) - Exodus 15:26

- **Jehovah-Shalom,** (The Lord our Peace) - Judges 6:24

- **Jehovah-Tsidkenu,** (The Lord Our Righteousness) - Jeremiah 23:6

- **Jehovah-Mekaddishkem,** (The Lord our Sanctifier) - Exodus 31:13

- **Jehovah-Sabaoth,** (The Lord of Hosts) - Isaiah 6:1-3

- **Jehovah-Shammah,** (The Lord is Present) - Ezekiel 48:35

- **Jehovah-Rohi,** (The Lord our Shepherd) - Psalm 23:1

- **Jehovah-Hoseenu,** (The Lord our Maker) - Psalm 95:6

- **Jehovah-Eloheenu,** (The Lord our God) - Psalm 99:7

- **El-Olam,** (God is Everlasting) - Isaiah 40:28-31

- **El-Roi,** (God is the Strong One) - Genesis 16:13.

CHAPTER 2

Experiencing God's Word

LET'S TALK ABOUT HOW we can experience God's Word in our daily life. We honor His name in all His creations.

We see He chooses us to learn His glorious works in the entire world. Recognize Him to know His Word.

He has planned an eternal life for us and to live with abundant joy. His presence covers the universe.

We breathe His Spirit. It is all about Him in all marvelous work on earth. Jesus is the center of all things.

Praise His holy name. The Spirit of God has completed the work in the universe.

Then we see God's Glory on every performance: nature, atmosphere, sun, moon, time, sky, cloud, wind, season, day, and night.

All creatures will have a purpose for living and to breathe God's spirit. The Word says that there is a time to be born and a time to die.

In all these things, God knew that His work succeeded very well. No one can create anything, except humans can discover them after God has created them first!

Let's ask the Lord to bring a revelation about His magnificent achievement. He shall reveal the purpose of our living on this earth.

He is watching us in every area of our personal lives and our ministry. There is a purpose in every prayer we seek Him and find Him.

Every person's cry with tears will be remembered. He is taking all our tears into His bottle.

"You number my wanderings;
Put my tears into Your bottle;
Are they not in Your book?" Psalm 56:8, NKJV.

Every act of tenderness toward others can be stacked up and stored up in heaven.

When we get there, God will open our Book of Life to see what we have done on earth. He is rewarding us here and in heaven, as well. Amen.

"The heavens declare the glory of God;
And the firmament shows His handiwork."
Psalm 19:1, NKJV.

Experiencing God:

The Word has commanded us to love God with all our hearts, to obey, to trust, to fear God, and to know Him more.

No place in the Bible that could be found will tell us to **"experience God."** But tell us to believe God by **'faith.'**

We find the word *'experience'* in the dictionary would explain to us; **"Taking part"** or participating.

Learning, knowing, acknowledging Him through the Word of God by experiencing His presence. Applying His Word which brings new Life to us.

Becoming a part of His Kingdom needed to have a new relationship to accept Jesus as Lord and Savior.

Then we are participating in the Glory of God and entering into His new life to encounter Him better.

The more studying and learning through His Word and the more we become strong in faith to receive the love of God.

The Spirit of God will open our understanding into the realm of spiritual revelation and wisdom.

All we have to do is to enter into His Word and accept Him who He is!

"by which have been given to us exceedingly great and precious promises, that through these you may be partakers of the divine nature, having escaped the corruption that is in the world through lust." 2 Peter 1:4, NKJV.

Created by Spoken Word:

I want to share the purpose of everything in the Bible. There will be a reason behind all existence around us.

Asking ourselves, where are all these things coming from? We look at it all with our own eyes.

Realizing the Almighty God has created everything for His pleasure. There is an authority in the work of God, and He gave us to enjoy His creation.

He wishes us to acknowledge His goodness and recognize that we have created nothing.

He has created everything for His splendor, and we use all His creation in our daily life. There is a purpose behind everything around us.

It even can be found in our houses and watching every material thing in every corner of our home.

We look at objects, touch things, use them for our needs, and we enjoy them. God has planned everything with a purpose.

When we go to the street and look at nature with green trees, then see cars. It's amazing to watch the sky, and it is a glorious work of God in heaven.

We are always living on this earth. Even though the Lord formed animals with incredible appearances and with an excellent design.

So, the purpose of His power is to create Life for every human and creature. It allows us to draw closer to Him.

The Word is Abundant Life:

Let's look at the meaning of **abundant life:** *'It's fullness of joy, and with peace of mind, body, and soul.'*

Learning from a lot of places in the Word of God encourages us. No matter what we have in the present life.

When we are dwelling in Christ, we will get a more abundant life with a cheerful and peaceful heart.

We should always remind ourselves that we are in Christ, and He resides in us. Therefore, we get a more abundant and everlasting life.

This verse said that the enemy is there to put us down. The devil came to steal our joy from us to kill our bodies, souls, and spirits.

Life in this world is very complicated. It's becoming harder to live in a peaceful environment, along with our families.

Because the Bible says that the thief came to steal our joy and peace. The enemy tries to give us false promises from every religion.

"The thief does not come except to steal, and to kill, and to destroy. I have come that they may

have life and that they may have it more abundantly." John 10:10, NKJV.

Jesus, our Eternal Salvation:

He is our eternal salvation that He is **the Life**. There is no other name that has been given to us to be saved through Him.

Here we understand that there is no other name that can be found under heaven to bring us salvation. His promise to us that we have a more abundant life.

No Salvation can be found by any other gods or in any books. Everyone is trying to introduce their gods to show us a way of life.

We watch people every day, how they are attached to new technology. You name it: **TV, computer, the internet, cellphone, social network, Computer Game.**

These techniques made such an impact on our lives that we feel we get lost in our salvation. And we don't know if we believe in the abundant life of Jesus or not?

With so many things taking effect around us, it is very confusing what to think now?

I wish everyone could be attached to the Lord and learn about the Fire of God.

"Nor is there salvation in any other, for there is no other name under heaven given among men by which we must be saved." Acts 12:4, NKJV.

Formed by Word:

God has established the entire world by the authority of His Word. The Holy Bible is not just a record of religious book writings.

Its messages of Law and Love of God are what the world is formed upon His spoken Words.

God is the author, builder, designer, planner, and architect of the world. He is a maker of Law, principles, and creator of all kinds of life on the earth.

His Glory and his rules are the groundwork of existence. If the framework is not there, the entire creation leads to failure, no means how wonderful will be.

In fact, His word, His creation cannot break down or nor never weaken. Because He is full of power and greatness.

He is in control of all things, and everything has been made for Himself. Amen.

Truthfulness Heart:

I wish to tell you why! It is because the Spirit lives in the Word of God called **"The Holy Bible."**

When we become born-again Christians, we receive a new spirit, and we accept Jesus by faith.

Then the Holy Spirit will enter into our hearts, and He dwells in our lives.

Because we have His Spirit, He will testify for us that Jesus is Lord. He is our **Everlasting Father**, and He is **Abundant Life**.

Only the Holy Spirit will reveal to us that other books cannot come from One true God. It may other people are representing their religions with a holy book.

In fact, they will try to reveal about their gods. But the Word tells us we must worship One true God with truthfulness heart.

The Holy Spirit will prove to us that other books and other gods do not have the Spirit of Truth.

This statement is very powerful; we believe He is our joy and peace and our eternal life. Amen.

"Read, Believe, Obey"

We desire to make our Christian life strong to have an experience of God's Word.

Three things we must pursue with a hungering heart.

- **Read the Word**
- **Believe the Word**
- **Obey the Word.**

We must remember there is power in the Word of God. As I mentioned before that everything has been established by spoken Word into existence.

If we don't experience the authority of God, that God's Word gives us the power to get saved.

He changes heart inside out, and He makes a new purpose for living. He gives confidence and freedom in our lives.

Personal Relationship:

There is actually every person's desire to make a personal relationship in getting to know Jesus.

When we spend time reading His Word, then faith will be rooted in our hearts.

Faith must be there to have a personal relationship with the Creator of the universe. We believe Jesus just as He knows us.

He transforms our hearts into marvelous life. He will enable us to live without sins with victory to glorify His name.

When we continue our lives concentrated on God, we encounter Him in our everyday lives. We understand His love and grace.

He gives us His peace and His presence. We learn to hear the voice of the Holy Spirit to comfort, teach, and guide us.

We contact Him in prayer. He provides for us every need. God wishes us to have His presence.

He loves to make us strong in faith to meditate in His Word. Let's glorify Him with singing, thanksgiving, and praise. Amen.

Hunger to be Filled:

The Lord loves to fill us with His Word, with His presence, and with His peace.

He is looking for those who are hungry to fill up their spirits with Fire.

He loves to see that we are walking in His Grace and living with the Fire of the Spirit.

We must have a desire to live and serve the people of God with His anointing.

We must have a deeper hunger for Him to read His Word and to pray in the spirit.

The Word mentioned: Out of every person's heart will flow rivers of living water.

Every person's heart would have hunger going after God. Humble heart shall be filled.

"He who believes in Me, as the Scripture has said, out of his heart will flow rivers of living water." John 7:38, NKJV.

At the same time, we get hungry in the spirit, and we feel we are empty inside.

So, we seek Him and read His Word to strengthen our spirit to become stronger.

Hunger for God is not exciting for many Christian believers in this generation.

Unfortunately, people are hungry for unnecessary material ambitions to bring them into darkness.

They will have temporary and short time pleasures. But those things draw them to confusion and a lost world without eternal life in Christ.

We are hungry for other things, and the things of the world are drawing us to sin, and we're getting lost in this world.

Hungry and Thirsty:

We need to turn our ambition around into a sincere desire to follow Him and run into the fire of the Holy Spirit.

Are we hungry or thirsty? I love this verse says that we must be thirsty and hungry for God.

I wish everyone could have a great passion for being hungry for His presence and thirst for His Word.

Because His Word is as a medicine in our body and to our soul and our spirit. His presence creates healing, and He perfects us for His glory.

"For He satisfies the longing soul,

And fills the hungry soul with goodness." Psalm 107:9, NKJV.

Shall be Filled:

This verse from the book of Matthew says that it blesses you to be hungry to know Him and seek Him for your life.

Our faith grows and builds up in our hearts by hearing Him and listening to His voice again.

We would always be ready to pray in season and out of season.

"Blessed are those who hunger and thirst for righteousness,

For they shall be filled." Matthew 5:6, NKJV.

I love the last phrase is! **"Shall be filled."** They shall be filled with the Holy Spirit and blessings and more miracles to come to us.

Are we ready to receive grace and the abundant kindness of the Lord?

He is pouring out from heaven to shower over us. Be ready to accept Him. in Jesus's name. Amen.

Knowing God through His Word:

The Word of God is eternal, and He breathes in us. **His Word is Life** to our spirit, soul, and body. The Word is His voice.

In the old days, the people didn't have any Bible to read about God.

They had to recognize the voice of God and His signs and wonders. Then the Lord has revealed Himself to His servant.

My favorite story is about Daniel in the Old Testament. This book is teaching us that Daniel had an intimacy with God.

"And I prayed to the Lord my God, and made confession, and said, "O Lord, great and awesome God, who keeps His covenant and mercy with those who love Him, and with those who keep His commandments." Daniel 9:4, NKJV.

He would declare any word of confession on behalf of the nation. He was very devoted to God and knowing God in a personal way.

God answered Daniel's prayer because he was walking in a purity and obedient life. He started to experience Him through God's voice.

Daniel discovered God through trust and believing in God's wonders. In fact, God had chosen Daniel to become a prophet in the time of exile in Babylon.

He saw visions and dreams for the future. Many believe that Daniel was a prayer warrior in his time.

I Am with you:

The Word of God is the eternal Word, which means when God Almighty has spoken already the Word to existence.

It shall be made and established forever. No one can have any authority to change the Word, He said, **"I Am with you."**

The moment we hear the voice of God and His spoken Word completed. As we look at the spiritual realm that He is fulfilling His Word and His promise.

Is He doing for us now? Yes. His presence is always in front of us, is behind us. He is on the left and right sides of us.

His love and His care are around us by His Spirit. Praise His holy name. Amen.

Spending Time in the Word:

The Lord wants us to seek Him. Spending time in the Word is a very effective way of praying in the spirit.

Telling Him in prayer, **"Lord, what would You have me to do every morning?"**

Teach me Your Will; show me how to grow up in memorizing Your Word.

The Lord loves it when we search for Him in our hearts. Acknowledge His way in every aspect and daily activities.

Learning His Word to become wiser and more knowledgeable. When we spend time in the Word and meditate in His presence.

Let's ask the Holy Spirit to fill us up with the fuel of God's Spirit. We would need to discipline ourselves, not to get distracted in other areas.

Needed Discipline:

The Lord is trying to teach and discipline us to come to God's presence regularly. There is a need to get our prayer in alignment with the Word of God.

He is teaching us from the leadership of the Spirit of the living God who has chosen us to pray.

The Lord has served us by His Spirit to instruct us and train us into the manifestation of victory.

We always desire to learn a new way in the Holy Spirit to be close to Him. Because of His love for us, to show His glorious plan.

He loves to discipline us with the most significant move of His anointing.

We can grow in prayer and become stronger warriors. We are especially humble in our Christian walk with Him.

An Intimate Relationship:

Discipline requires a personal dedication to have an intimate relationship with the Holy Spirit.

He helps to make a change from a bad habit in a good manner. I mean, some of the things we are used to doing, would not help us have a great time in prayer.

God wants to set an example for others that they can learn more about His greatness.

It's needed to look at some areas in our daily devotion, where is a lack of growth in the Word.

It's so good to have intimacy in the Spirit and with our loved ones.

Let's check where we are lacking so we can engage in our communication with Him. It would lead us to make significant confidence in the Lord.

Experiencing God with Scriptures:

- **Victory in midst of troubles.**
  "My brethren, count it all joy when you fall into various trials, knowing that the testing of your faith produces patience.
  But let patience have *its* perfect work, that you may be perfect and complete, lacking nothing." James 1:2-4, NKJV.
- **Living fruitfulness lives with joy.**
  "But the fruit of the Spirit is love, joy, peace, longsuffering, kindness, goodness,

faithfulness, gentleness, self-control. Against such, there is no law." Galatians 5:22-23, NKJV.

- **Give our thoughts in God's will.**
  "Therefore gird up the loins of your mind, be sober, and rest *your* hope fully upon the grace that is to be brought to you at the revelation of Jesus Christ." 1 Peter 1:13, NKJV.

- **The Presence of the Holy Spirit.**
  "Or do you not know that your body is the temple of the Holy Spirit *who is* in you, whom you have from God, and you are not your own?

  For you were bought at a price; therefore glorify God in your body and in your spirit, which are God's." 1 Corinthians 6:19-20, NKJV.

- **The Lord directs our steps.**
  "A man's heart plans his way, But the Lord directs his steps." Proverbs 16:9, NKJV.

- **The Lord gives us rest in His Presence.**
  "For we who have believed do enter that rest, as He has said: "So I swore in My wrath, **'They shall not enter My rest,'**" although the works were finished from the foundation of the world." Hebrews 4:3, NKJV.

- **All things are possible.**

  "But He said, the things which are impossible with men are possible with God." Luke 18:27, NKJV.

- **God loves us.**

  "For God so loved the world that He gave His only begotten Son, that whoever believes in Him should not perish but have everlasting life." John 3:16, NKJV.

- **The Lord forgives us.**

  "There is therefore now no condemnation to those who are in Christ Jesus, who do not walk according to the flesh, but according to the Spirit." Romans 8:1, NKJV.

- **All things work together for good.**

  "And we know that all things work together for good to those who love God, to those who are the called according to His purpose." Romans 8:28, NKJV.

- **We receive wisdom from God.**

  "But of Him you are in Christ Jesus, who became for us wisdom from God—and righteousness and sanctification and redemption." 1 Corinthians 1:30, NKJV.

- **God is able.**

  "And God is able to make all grace abound toward you, that you, always having all sufficiency in all things, may have an abundance for every good work." 2 Corinthians 9:8, NKJV.

- **God's grace is sufficient for us.**

  "And He said to me, "My grace is sufficient for you, for My strength is made perfect in weakness." Therefore most gladly I will rather boast in my infirmities, that the power of Christ may rest upon me." 2 Corinthians 12:9, NKJV.

CHAPTER 3

The Word Saves Us

FROM THE BEGINNING OF creation, God has given all men a free choice to choose Life.

Because of man's disobedient and wrong decisions, he separates himself from God and man fell into sin.

Every man has decided to disobey God's authority. Adam and Eve have sinned by disobeying God in the Garden of Eden.

When they transgressed against God's Word, which has spoken to them, their relationship with God was broken.

They had experienced spiritual death, in which they were separated from God's presence. Then the spirit of sin passed on to every generation.

God had a plan to make a relationship with the world. He's provided salvation through His Son Jesus, and He should come to die for our sins.

God had reached out His love from heaven to a lost world. When Jesus came to earth as the Son of God, He had full authority in heaven.

He came to earth to achieve the glorious act of atonement and redemption once for all.

The Son of God should die to save us from our sins. We see God's justice and His Grace had been made possible in order to be forgiven.

He made the only way to reconcile with us by His Love and His mercy.

We recognize His willingness to restore us and make a new relationship with the Father again. It's one of the important statements of Christianity.

Sin Causes Death:

Sin lives in us and leads to eternal death. It makes us to unable to go in God's presence.

How amazing is that God made us have a relationship with Him? Because of His righteousness, and He is Holy.

There are no sinful creatures that may allow entering into God's presence. Sin causes us, not to have a perfect relationship with our Creator.

We were created for Him to worship and adore Him. We cannot save ourselves, and it's impossible to get freed from spiritual death on our own.

"for all have sinned and fall short of the glory of God." Romans 3:23, NKJV.

Free Choice to Life:

All humans have been created for eternity. God sincerely loves for us to accept eternity with Him. He allows us to choose Life and to make a decision for ourselves.

Even though He loves all His creations. When we choose to sin, which draws us into the darkness of life.

But His goodness will never leave us. His holiness, purity, and righteousness brought a new life through Jesus.

The blood of Jesus can cleanse all sins of the world. Rejoicing in His mercy shall be our gifts of life.

"Righteousness and justice are the foundation of Your throne; Mercy and truth go before Your face." Psalm 89:14, NKJV.

Sinless Jesus:

Jesus was sinless because He was not born through human contact. The **"First Adam"** brought sin into the world.

But the **"second Adam, Jesus."** He took the sins of the world. Instead, we should be punished, because of our own sins.

God sent Jesus to die a harsh death on a cross. God condemned and judged the entire world by giving Jesus for us. Glory to His name.

There was the wrath of God that came upon Jesus to cover us from the darkness. The misery of sins we get and then came over sinless Jesus.

He said in His last breath, **"It is finished."** Let's rejoice that the sins of the world have paid been in full. Amen.

"And so it is written,
"The first man Adam became a living being."
The last Adam became a life-giving spirit.

However, the spiritual is not first, but the natural, and afterward the spiritual. The first man was
of the earth, made of dust; *the second Man is the Lord
from heaven."* 1 Corinthians 15:45-48, NKJV.

The Wages of Sin is Death:

When sin entered into the world and there is no
way to remove sins from the human's life.

There will be punishment for sinning against
God, it is spiritual death.

There was only God Himself was able to remove
sin and death by giving His only begotten Son.

So, Jesus accepted punishment for all of us.
Bringing mankind into a new relationship with God
by faith.

God saw there was no Life and hope for all humanity. The main reasons God spoke the Word.

As we know, the Word is Jesus, and the Father
sent Him into the world. Without Him, all humans
will experience eternal suffering.

God acknowledged Jesus' sacrifice on the cross of
Calvary for our sins on our behalf!

The gift of salvation is available for everyone who
will receive Jesus as Lord and Savior by faith.

"For the wages of sin is death, but the gift of God is eternal life in Christ Jesus our Lord." Romans 6:23, NKJV.

Confession of Faith:

- Jesus will abide in me.

  "Abide in Me, and I in you. As the branch cannot bear fruit of itself, unless it abides in the vine, neither can you, unless you abide in Me." John 15:4, NKJV.

- Jesus will walk with me.

  "As you therefore have received Christ Jesus the Lord, so walk in Him." Colossians 2:6, NKJV.

- Jesus will speak with me.

  "Then you will call upon Me and go and pray to Me, and I will listen to you.

  And you will seek Me and find Me, when you search for Me with all your heart." Jeremiah 29:12-13, NKJV.

- Jesus will direct my path.

  "Your word is a lamp to my feet. And a light to *my path*." Psalm 119:105, NKJV.

- Jesus will be my friend.

  "No longer do I call you servants, for a servant does not know what his master is doing; but *I have called you friends*, for all things that I heard from My Father I have made known to you." John 15:15, NKJV.

- Jesus will give me rest.

  "There remains therefore *a rest for the people of God.* For he who has entered *His rest* has himself also ceased from his works as God did from His." Hebrews 4:9-10, NKJV.

- Jesus will strengthen me.

  "The Lord is my strength and my shield; My heart trusted in Him, and I am helped; Therefore my heart greatly rejoices." Psalm 28:7, NKJV.

- Jesus will answer me.

  "Call to Me, and I will answer you, and show you great and mighty things, which you do not know." Jeremiah 33:3, NKJV.

- Jesus is with me.

  "What then shall we say to these things? If God is for us, who can be against us?" Romans 8:31, NKJV.

- Jesus will never fail me.

  "Has His mercy ceased forever? Has His promise failed forevermore?" Psalm 77:8, NKJV.

- Jesus loves me.

  "But God demonstrates His own love toward us, in that while we were still sinners, Christ died for us." Romans 5:8, NKJV.

Impossible to Earn Salvation:

We all are trying to earn salvation by our good work or by being pleasant people. God has brought salvation, which is the free gift of God.

When we hear the Word, then we receive Jesus by faith. We need faith to believe in our hearts that Jesus is the Savior.

He can bring redemption and freedom only. It was impossible to please God without faith.

There is no way for the sinner to perform the law of God. As we recognize that God is **Holy, Just, and Love.**

If we repent of our sins and ask God to forgive us, He cleans us as well.

If Jesus did not die and be resurrected from the dead. There is no salvation for us.

God is able to restore our sinful lifestyle to a new life of Jesus. He can change us from nothing to something better.

We witness the way of salvation to the world, and we call the good news must be proclaimed.

The word prepares us with a powerful message to preach to lost souls.

Sharing the Gospel by His Authority:

As we recognize, God is the authority, and we as the believer in Christ are under God's sovereignty.

God gave them power and authority to His Son, Jesus. Then He gave it to us to do the work of the Kingdom of God. And He came and spoke to them, saying,

"All authority has been given to Me in heaven and on earth." Matthew 28:18, NKJV.

He brought the power to us as part of our inheritance in Christ. Glory to His name.

We know when the believer gives his life to Christ; we receive all authority from the Lord.

The Holy Spirit moves into our lives to anoint us with power. The authority comes from God and is from the Word.

The authority of Christ gives the legal right that we declare we are a child of God.

We share the Gospel; we speak His love and His grace. We will witness His salvation by His authority.

Justification by Faith:

We read from the book of Galatians said: *'Knowing that a man is not justified by the works of the law.'*

What is the Justification by faith in the Bible? It means **'being declared righteous in Christ.'**

It's involved a powerful work of God in the Bible. It represents the act of God with His love in which He claims that a man is not guilty.

We are justified because of the Lord Jesus. The Word said, we don't need to work hard and try to earn forgiveness.

There is not a requirement to accomplish more of God's law. It's needed to have faith to receive all God's love, grace, and mercy.

So, Jesus justifies us. Therefore, we belong to God and live a blessed life.

"knowing that a man is not justified by the works of the law but by faith in Jesus Christ, even we have believed in Christ Jesus, that we might be justified by faith in Christ and not by the works of the law; for by the works of the law no flesh shall be justified." Galatians 2:16, NKJV.

Preaching the Word from the Book of Acts:

Studying the book of Acts, we see Jesus's disciples preached the Word by the power of the Gospel which edifies and inspires us.

As the Word will spread throughout the world and transform many lives.

The Lord has given many wonders during this season of revival by the apostles to confirm their messages.

It's come to know about the apostolic signs and miracles. It was God's presence in their messages through these men of God.

The book of Acts reveals how God actually has chosen a group of fishermen and many ordinary men.

The Lord used them to change the world. God can accomplish marvelous works through simple people.

Then the Holy Spirit comes down with fire, and the Lord Jesus empowers them through His presence.

Unmerited Favor:

Today we will experience the Grace of God. Let's look at the meaning of the word **"Grace."**

According to Christian theologians and scholars means **"unmerited favor."**

The understanding of Grace is far from our minds what our Father in Heaven has done for the entire world.

None of us deserves to get saved because we are all sinned. There is no way out of this life unless to believe in the Son of God.

The Lord carried out a plan to bring us out of sinful life into a new life of blessings. So, the choice is ours, to make the right decision.

Something is better than our own faith. The Lord requires us to have faith in Him and His Word to receive everlasting life.

Sins produce pain, sorrow, and sickness, with eternal death without salvation.

Trusting in God's Word:

I believe in the authority of God given to us through Jesus. The life of believers must be depending on the Word of the Lord.

We can do nothing without His spirit and His presence. His power and His authority make new transforming life.

He is carrying out a fresh way of life for us. We, as new creations in Christ, should trust in God's Word.

The believer's heart must have true confidence in God's power. According to the Great Commission of Jesus, He gave us the authority of His name.

To His children, to followers, to ministers, to servants, and essentially to all his believers.

We can carry His Word with the authority of the Holy Spirit. We can reach out to lost souls and bring them into the Kingdom of God.

New Life in Christ:

The Grace of God will come into our lives with a new spirit and new life in Christ. We need to have a new creation and to have the word of authority.

Our mindset will be to look at the victory of Jesus, and the blood of the Lamb of God will cover our sins.

We are forgiven and healed in Jesus' name. We are the mighty believer in authority to bind and rebuke the devil's territory.

We must lie down in our former selves to be renewed as a new identity in Christ.

When we welcome the Holy Spirit to come into our lives, and He changes us daily.

But we must be determined to allow Him to work in us. God knows our hearts, and He never discouraged us and hurt us.

He chooses us, and He loves to take care of our needs. We must apply the Word of God to restore and renew our minds.

We recognize ourselves with a new man in Christ, which He has established us in righteousness and true holiness.

Committed Forgiving our Sins:

God has committed to forgiving the sins of those who are in the new covenant. Therefore, new life in Christ has two main aspects.

An inner part of spiritual renewal appears in a fresh relationship with the Lord Jesus.

Then, by inviting Jesus as Lord and Savior into our hearts with new faith, we are a new creation in Christ.

When Jesus arrived to finish the plan of God. He died on the cross, and He rose again from the dead.

Therefore, we will no longer be under the Law. The Grace of God took place by Jesus, winning the victory.

The Old Covenant has given for which everything remained. Now we praise God that Jesus has taken over with a better covenant as King of Kings.

Now He is the Savior, which he is the advocate of the old one. Since He provides a new life to come and dwell in our spirit.

"But now He has obtained a more excellent ministry, inasmuch as He is also Mediator of a better

covenant, which was established on better promises." Hebrews 8:6, NKJV.

God's Salvation with Scriptures:

- **Jesus is the only way to salvation.**
  "Nor is there salvation in any other, for there
  is no other name under heaven given among
  men by which we must be saved." Acts 4:12,
  NKJV.
- **Work out our own salvation with fear and
  trembling.**
  "Therefore, my beloved, as you have always
  obeyed, not as in my presence only, but now
  much more in my absence, work out your
  own salvation with fear and trembling."
  Philippians 2:12, NKJV.
- **Jesus is our sinless and perfect sacrifice.**
  "but with the precious blood of Christ, as of
  a lamb without blemish and without spot." 1
  Peter 1:19, NKJV.
- **Jesus paid the penalty for our sin.**
  "But God demonstrates His own love toward
  us, in that while we were still sinners, Christ
  died for us." Romans 5:8, NKJV.

- **Receiving Salvation by Grace through faith.**

  "For by grace you have been saved through faith, and that not of yourselves; *it is* the gift of God, not of works, lest anyone should boast." Ephesians 2:8-9, NKJV.

- **Follow Jesus and carry His cross daily.**

  "Then He said to *them* all, "If anyone desires to come after Me, let him deny himself, and take up his cross daily, and follow Me." Luke 9:23, NKJV.

- **I am justified by the blood of Jesus, saved from God's wrath.**

  "Much more then, having now been justified by His blood, we shall be saved from wrath through Him." Romans 5:9, NKJV.

- **Salvation belongs to the Lord.**

  "Salvation belongs to the Lord. Your blessing is upon Your people. Selah." Psalm 3:8, NKJV.

- **The salvation of the righteous.**

  "But the salvation of the righteous is from the Lord; He is their strength in the time of trouble." Psalm 37:39, NKJV.

- **My salvation comes from Him.**

  "Truly my soul silently waits for God; From Him comes my salvation." Psalm 62:1, NKJV.

- **The rock of my salvation.**

  "He shall cry to Me, 'You are my Father, My God, and the rock of my salvation.'" Psalm 89:26, NKJV.

- **Jesus is the way, the truth, and the life.**

  "Jesus said to him, "I am the way, the truth, and the life. No one comes to the Father except through Me." John 14:6, NKJV.

- **I am not ashamed of the gospel of Christ.**

  "For I am not ashamed of the gospel of Christ, for it is the power of God to salvation for everyone who believes, for the Jew first and also for the Greek." Romans 1:16, NKJV.

- **The right to become children of God.**

  "But as many as received Him, to them He gave the right to become children of God, to those who believe in His name: who were born, not of blood, nor of the will of the flesh, nor of the will of man, but of God." John 1:12-13, NKJV.

- **The word of truth, the gospel of your salvation.**

  "In Him you also trusted, after you heard the word of truth, the gospel of your salvation; in whom also, having believed, you were sealed with the Holy Spirit of promise, who is the guarantee of our inheritance until the redemption of the purchased possession, to the praise of His glory." Ephesians 1:13-14, NKJV.

- **Must be a born-again Christian.**

  "Jesus answered and said to him, "Most assuredly, I say to you, unless one is born again, he cannot see the kingdom of God." John 3:3, NKJV.

- **For the grace of God that brings salvation.**

  "For the grace of God that brings salvation has appeared to all men." Titus 2:11, NKJV.

- **To obtain salvation through our Lord Jesus.**

  "For God did not appoint us to wrath, but to obtain salvation through our Lord Jesus Christ, who died for us, that whether we wake or sleep, we should live together with Him." 1 Thessalonians 5:9-10, NKJV.

CHAPTER 4

The Word Transforms Us

THERE IS A MIGHTY power in the Word to transform us. One of the major things in the Word of God is encouraging us to live for the Lord.

To continue carrying out His name in our lives. Because the Spirit of God is alive and active to save, heal the sick, and perform many great miracles.

The Spirit of Living God cannot exist in any other books in the world to be compared with the Bible.

The reason God gave us His Word is to transfer us into an image of His Son, Jesus. So that our characters will become stronger to manifest Jesus.

Though, we believe that God's Word has been given to us to get transformed into an image of Jesus. Then we realize why we desire to become a new person.

He has formed us in the likeness of Jesus. He made us to revealing His grace through our thankfulness, worship, and adoration.

The Word is a Weapon:

The Word is a weapon for spiritual rebirth, restoration, regeneration, redemption, and more…

We look at the dignity of Jesus and God's Love surely is in the Bible. It reveals to us how our God has done for us.

We must worship Him in the spirit and truth. The Bible will describe God's power and how He can change us to make us like Jesus.

The whole purpose of the Word is to demonstrate **the image of Jesus.**

When we open up our Bible, we discover the entire Words of God are speaking about Jesus. As we recognize, **Jesus is the center of the Bible.**

God will transform us so that we can be a witness of Jesus to bring others in the knowledge of His Glory. Amen.

From Trust to Victory:

His Word is here in our hearts to manifest His authority. We're believing and declaring His name.

Claiming His Word will encourage us to build up our faith to higher levels of maturity.

It is very important to rely on His Word and depend on the leadership of the Holy Spirit.

But we have some issues of trust; we see some Christians have a weakness in their trust in the Lord.

We believe the Word: we decree His promise and declare it over every situation. You may say, "I have done all these things, but nothing is happening.

We wait upon the Lord with the peace of God. Waiting is a hard thing for everyone; we want an answer now.

I believe the Word is powerful, and there is no error in the truth of God.

We lay down all our petitions before the Lord. We declare **"the name of Jesus"** for victory.

Change Us to Become Strong:

The word of God encourages us to be transferred into mighty men and women of God.

God formed us to become Godly believers to glorify Jesus. As we determine to improve our lives based on God's knowledge and His wisdom.

He promises us in His Word, there is an authority in the Word of God to make strong faith in our lives.

God expects us to have a strong faith. Not giving up very easily in any situation.

When we are involved with unknown circumstances, and we don't know what to do?

Therefore, we know His Word, and He promised to lead us to victory in a peaceful manner.

Abiding in His Word is very vital, and He will never fail us. He will find a way to take us through the rough times in life.

Because by surrounding ourselves under His authority. He develops our spiritual living and changes us more like Jesus.

The Word requires us to grow in the grace to become mature and live under His power. Amen.

Transform Us:

Let's try to live according to the Word of God. We don't have to desire to follow the pleasures of the world.

There is no need to duplicate the style and manners of daily culture. Let us allow God to change us into a new character by developing our new nature.

Then we will understand, recognizing God's will, which is excellent and accurate.

Surrendering ourselves under the plan of God to obey God's Word as living sacrifices.

We have to do an important act on our part to ignore the unnecessary sinful desire.

We must be determined to reject the things of a corrupted daily lifestyle.

Therefore, we will be ready to discern and pursue God's will alone. Let God makes us into a new character by adjusting the way we think.

Transformation doesn't take place immediately, but it carries a successful process of life without sins.

He will help us to sanctify ourselves by His own spirit and His Word and make us Holy.

We will continue to trust Him and walk by faith in the Lord.

He is renewing our minds, our hearts daily and to become strong by His power in His Word. Amen.

"I beseech you therefore, brethren, by the mercies of God, that you present your bodies a living sacrifice, holy, acceptable to God, which is your reasonable service." Romans 12:1, NJKV.

He Converts Every Soul:

The Good News of Jesus is making marvelous transformations in every life. He is performing the changes with no one's help.

Even He is not getting any permission to do the miracles. He is doing it because of His love for us. He is converting one soul after another to save lives.

He wants to turn individual hearts to bring back to Himself. He receives all honor in the name of Jesus.

When someone gets saved and to see a loved one changed in the Light of Jesus.

We are rejoicing and speaking aloud with the joy of the Lord, saying, **"Hallelujah, Praise the Lord."**

Turn Around our Situation:

The Bible says that if we accept Him, He will acknowledge us to the Father. We must allow Him to turn our situation around to a new way of God.

It might be in a condition where we think there is no hope. Having thought about all of our confidence is dead.

Then we ask Him in prayer, **"Lord, resurrect my problem and turn it into a new future."**

Bringing praise and glory in your name. This should be a good prayer for us.

Confidence in His Ability:

We say with great confidence. **"Have your way,"** Lord, I will back up, and I allow You to step forward.

When He moves ahead, then we walk behind Him. Say aloud, I am trusting You. I believe in You to prepare away for me.

Lord, You always work a great job. I am waiting for you to turn around my condition.

Sometimes we must be honest with ourselves to ask Him. I am tired of doing my own way. I repent my sins to you. Please forgive me.

I promise not to try to fix my problem and my situation. But I will submit my life in your hand.

Teach me, O Lord, **"I trust in Your Word, Your ability, and Your power."** It is our confession to the Lord.

Transforming to a New Thing:

We must tell Him in our prayer, "I am weak, but You are strong. The transformations of my situation will take place in Your name."

Then, we'll begin to testify to what the Lord has done. We receive fresh excitement from the Spirit of the Lord.

When we share the mercy of the Lord everywhere, what the Lord has done.

Because of His grace that He is increasing the love of the Father into prayer, and He shall answer it.

From Weak to Strong:

Allow our mentality and the way of our thinking to change. God is a life changer. We should be cheerful witnesses.

Tell everybody around us what the Lord has done for us. In fact, if we will not get any changes in our situation right away now.

He remained faithful to change our circumstances in His time. Our testimony will be a great impact on many people around us.

People were always saying in the old days, **"Chill out! He is doing it soon for us."** Amen.

"Therefore, I take pleasure in infirmities, in reproaches, in needs, in persecutions, in distresses, for Christ's sake. For when I am weak, then I am strong." 2 Corinthians 12:10, NKJV.

Transformed into Humility:

Humility is rewarding to lay our lives down in the presence of the Lord.

It requires learning from the Lord to be disciplined and getting to know more about His anointing.

His presence will humble us in prayer; then, we grow in worship.

The more we understand about the brokenness of the heart, and the more we're growing in the Word.

We step up into triumph in prayer life. The Holy Spirit is ready to move us into God's glory.

He will guide us into all truth, and it will be magnificent in the spirit realm.

If we sometimes feel lonely, there is no one listening to our prayer. We don't need to think we are alone.

That's the moment we encounter the Lord watching, and He is surrounding us with all blessings.

When we call upon the Lord, He is here in the midst of His people.

We say aloud, **"Holy Spirit, I humble myself before you, and I will surrender all to you."**

Submitting is the hardest thing in our lives. Jesus surrounded himself under the Father's plan.

He desires to see that we all yield to Him with a humble spirit, and we pick up His cross to follow Him.

We will not be ashamed of His name. He is leading us on a great path. The light of Jesus is shining on our future.

A broken heart is about humility in His presence. Are you ready to give yourself to enter His heavenly throne?

Ask the Holy Spirit to lead you with peace and a fresh revelation. He will exalt the humble into a remarkable achievement. In the name of Jesus. Amen.

"The Lord is near to those who have a broken heart,

And saves such as have a contrite spirit." Psalm 34:18, NKJV.

Prayer of Agreement:

The prayer of agreement is very important to seek the Lord along with others.

The power of the Holy Spirit will be there to manifest God's fire in the church.

It becomes very easy for us because we won't force ourselves to pray. The Holy Spirit will give us peace and joy to continue to move forward.

Then the anointing of the Lord continues to pour down in the place to hear God's voice.

We realize God is releasing His power with love and peace on us.

This powerful statement is about the prayer of agreement. It makes a difference. Amen.

"Again, I say to you that if two of you agree on earth concerning anything that they ask, it will be done for them by My Father in heaven." Matthew 18:19, NKJV.

Story of Transformation:

There is a beautiful story of the woman, Mary who anointed the feet of Jesus with the oil. She came to the Lord; she was bowing down.

Basically, she laid down her life with a humble spirit to wash Jesus's feet.

She surrendered her humbleness and her faith to the degree that she started to worship Him.

She didn't even look at Jesus; her head was down to begin ministering to the Lord.

We don't have any explanation of what happened after she left the presence of the Lord; something shifted her life to a new life of victory.

She may have changed everything around her city, and maybe she created her own ministry.

When we have a perfect experience with His touch, His healing, and forgiveness. It will transform our hearts, and we will not be the same again.

"Then Mary took a pound of very costly oil of spikenard, anointed the feet of Jesus, and wiped His feet with her hair. And the house was filled with the fragrance of the oil." John 12:3, NKJV.

God's Transformation with Scriptures:

- **Living for Jesus only.**
  "I have been crucified with Christ; it is no longer I who live, but Christ lives in me; and the *life* which I now live in the flesh I live by faith in the Son of God, who loved me and gave Himself for me." Galatians 2:20, NKJV.
- **Walking worthy of the Lord.**
  "that you may walk worthy of the Lord, fully pleasing Him, being fruitful in every good work and increasing in the knowledge of God." Colossians 1:10, NKJV.

- **Do all to the glory of God.**

  "Therefore, whether you eat or drink, or whatever you do, do all to the glory of God." 1 Corinthians 10:31, NKJV.

- **Glorify God in your body and your spirit.**

  "For you were bought at a price; therefore glorify God in your body and in your spirit, which are God's." 1 Corinthians 6:20, NKJV.

- **Honor the Lord.**

  "Honor the Lord with your possessions, And with the firstfruits of all your increase." Proverbs 3:9, NKJV.

- **We are a new creation in Christ.**

  "Therefore, if anyone is in Christ, he is a new creation; old things have passed away; behold, all things have become new." 2 Corinthians 5:17, NKJV.

- **Transformed from glory to glory.**

  "But we all, with unveiled face, beholding as in a mirror the glory of the Lord, are being transformed into the same image *from glory to glory*, just as by the Spirit of the Lord." 2 Corinthians 3:18, NKJV.

- **All grace abounds toward us.**

   "And God is able to make all grace abound toward you, that you, always having all sufficiency in all things, may have an abundance for every good work." 2 Corinthians 9:8, NKJV.

- **Renewing of our minds.**

   "And do not be conformed to this world, but be transformed by the renewing of your mind, that you may prove what is that good and acceptable and perfect will of God." Romans 12:2, NKJV.

CHAPTER 5

The Promise of God's Word

THERE ARE MANY POWERFUL promises of God in which we discover in the Bible.

Looking at all assurances of God's Word in this chapter. When we are going through an insecure situation in our lives.

God never breaks His promise, He is always standing on His Word. He said: *I am ready to perform my Word.* I just reminded of the verse:

"Then the Lord said to me, "You have seen well, for I am ready to perform My word." Jeremiah 1:12, NKJV.

To Bless Abraham:

God has promised to bless Abraham and to increase his descendants. It's called the **Abrahamic Covenant** is the endless, unchangeable, everlasting promises.

God established His relationship with Abraham that was made with the Jewish people.

This promise is an everlasting covenant, which continues into the forthcoming kingdom of Christ. It took place in the coming of **Messiah.**

"Your father Abraham rejoiced to see My day, and he saw it and was glad." John 8:56, NKJV.

Abraham Descendants:

God promised Abraham a son who would be the heir of the covenant. God formed a nation that would multiply over the face of the earth.

It's a Covenant of agreement, **"binding together"** a relationship based upon promises.

God established that one of those descendants would be a blessing to all the nations of the world.

According to the Law, as it was said, Abraham was the first Jew; he was also called a Hebrew.

He would become a father of nations; his descendants would be as numerous as the stars.

The Lord will bless all the nations of the earth through Abraham, Isaac, and Jacob.

"Get out of your country,

From your family

And from your father's house,

To a land that I will show you.

I will make you a great nation;

I will bless you, And make your name great;

And you shall be a blessing.

I will bless those who bless you,

And I will curse him who curses you;

And in you all the families of the earth shall be blessed." Genesis 12:1-3, NKJV.

Promised a Son:

This is an encouraging word for us. We can take into our spirit as we meditate on the Word of God and His goodness.

Abraham thought the promise of God would be impossible to get fulfilled. Because he was 100 years and Sarah was 90 years old.

He made a wrong decision to rush quickly into conceiving a son with Hagar, who was not chosen by God. She was a servant of Abraham's wife, Sarah.

A son was born through Hagar; she named him Ishmael. He became the father of the modern Arab nations. Abraham might have asked himself.

If God had promised him a son from which He would make a great nation, where was the son?

He was old, and Sarah was also an older woman. How could it be possible, and where would a son come from?

I believe God encouraged him by saying, **"I am a miracle-working God."**

If Sarah is 90 years old, I can still make her young with a new womb to carry a child.

What God did in this situation can be a great re-assurance to us today.

God can make a miracle, and no one can create miracles as He can! **God's promise will never fail.**

Watch over Israel:

God promised to His people, Israel, to be their God. He will make a great nation for His own, to lead and to watch over them.

We see in the Old Testament is recorded with many powerful fulfilling of His commitment. His promise is still existing to this day.

"I will walk among you and be your God, and you shall be My people. I am the Lord your God, who brought you out of the land of Egypt, that you should not be their slaves; I have broken the bands of your yoke and made you walk upright." Leviticus 26:12-13, NKJV.

His Promise for Salvation:

There is a promise that God establishes with mankind. He makes an agreement that He will forgive sin.

He will restore His relationship with those hearts that are changed toward Him.

There is the mediator who is Jesus, coming into the world by the Salvation of God to save humanity.

Jesus' death on the cross is the evidence of His promise. The New Covenant requires a complete transformation of heart, soul, spirit, and mind.

It will take place so that God's people are easily gratifying onto Him. It has also declared the message of the New Covenant.

He Saved Us:

God promised salvation, redemption, and restoration from our sins. Faith shall save us to those who believe in the Son of God, Jesus.

This is a free gift of God's salvation. God promises to redeem us by His mercy. He is holy and righteous, and we are living in sin.

God saw every sin that we were committed and made into corrupted shameful desire. We are fallen in this life, which God has given to us.

But we were dying in the spirit, soul, and body. Because we were sinners, Jesus, the Son of God, came to redeem us.

We should pay our own penalty for our sins. Having rebellion against God, but God has restored us by His Grace.

"He has delivered us from the power of darkness and conveyed us into the kingdom of the Son of His love, in whom we have redemption through His blood, the forgiveness of sins." Colossians 1:13-14, NKJV.

Promised to Forgive Us:

God promised us to forgive us when we confess our sins and any mistake done in life.

He is faithful to love and helps us to walk in the righteousness of God. The Lord can build up our spiritual lives into a glorious future.

He will bring peace and care for our needs. He is able to forget our past.

When we receive Jesus as our savior by faith and declare Jesus as our personal Lord. I believe the Word of God will restore us.

There will not be any judgment and condemnation for those who believe in the Lord.

He will be taking care of our lives and we live under His blessings.

"If we confess our sins, He is faithful and just to forgive us our sins and to cleanse us from all unrighteousness." 1 John 1:9, NKJV.

Promised Eternal Life:

Eternal life is promised to all who believe in Jesus as the Son of God. They believe that God raised Jesus from the dead.

Jesus promised everlasting life to those who are living according to His Word and trust in Him. This is the highest assurance of all.

"He who believes in the Son has everlasting life; and he who does not believe the Son shall not see life, but the wrath of God abides on him." John 3:36, NKJV.

Heavenly Blessings:

God promised to all Christians to those who are saved and born-again to have every spiritual blessing in Christ.

"Blessed be the God and Father of our Lord Jesus Christ, who has blessed us with every spiritual

blessing in the heavenly places in Christ." Ephesians 1:3, NKJV.

We, as the church today, have been promised and reserved our heavenly blessings for us.

"to an inheritance incorruptible and undefiled and that does not fade away, reserved in heaven for you." 1 Peter 1:4, NKJV.

The Holy Spirit Came:

Jesus promised to send the Holy Spirit after He ascended to Heaven and sitting at the right hand of the Father.

We see the Lord Jesus has been fulfilled His Word on the Day of Pentecost. So, the Holy Spirit is a gift for the church.

"But you shall receive power when the Holy Spirit has come upon you; and you shall be witnesses to Me in Jerusalem, and in all Judea and Samaria, and to the end of the earth." Acts 1:8, NKJV.

His Return:

When Jesus ascended to heaven, He promised us that He would come back soon.

This is a day called; **Rapture** and **'catching up'** of all Christians to heaven to live with Him in His heavenly Kingdom.

We are experiencing now in our Christian faith that we are waiting for His Second Coming of the Lord to the earth.

We, as Christian believers can agree that Jesus is coming back. The Word said: we must be ready to Day of His Return.

Living and walking by faith to victory in life. So, that He may say **"well done, and faithful servant."**

He will reward us on a glorious day when we meet King Jesus face to face. Amen.

"Behold, I tell you a mystery: We shall not all sleep, but we shall all be changed, in a moment, in the twinkling of an eye, at the last trumpet.

For the trumpet will sound, and the dead will be raised incorruptible, and we shall be changed." 1 Corinthians 15:51-52, NKJV.

Provision for Our Needs:

God promised to provide all our needs according to His Word. He assures us that we receive with the overflow of financial abundance.

He cares for our daily provision. But the Lord Jesus knows all our desires and He will be taken care of them.

"And my God shall supply all your need according to His riches in glory by Christ Jesus." Philippians 4:19, NKJV.

He Never Forsakes Us:

God promised us to not forsake us. The moment we accept Jesus in our hearts, we belong to Him.

Anyone who has felt ever rejected by God or from someone else. We should have a heart in the promise of our Father. He will never give up on us.

I would say, let us trust the Word of God. Therefore, we can be steadfast and strong in the spirit.

God will deliver us from every difficult situation. He will bring light into the dark hour of our lives.

We can call upon the Lord and He will fight our battles for his name's sake. His promise is always the truth. Amen.

Devil attacks, We Resist him:

The Lord promised us to give us victory when we are going through a tough time.

When we are living a Christian life, there will be a lot of temptation comes around us.

I believe the Lord will teach us to resist the devil and he will flee from us.

Speak the Word to every devil attack and we can free from all negative thoughts.

The Lord will protect and give peace in our situations.

"Therefore submit to God. Resist the devil and he will flee from you." James 4:7, NKJV.

He Started a New Life:

God promised to accomplish the work in our lives which He began a new life.

God does not leave His work halfway. He started the work in us, and He will finish it.

"being confident of this very thing, that He who has begun a good work in you will complete it until the day of Jesus Christ." Philippians 1:6, NKJV.

Strength to the Weak:

We don't know what is happening in our daily lives, but we can call upon the Lord. He promises us to release His **"strength to the weak."**

"He gives power to the weak,
And to those who have no might
He increases strength." Isaiah 40:29, NKJV.

He Redeemed Us:

God is holy, and we are living in sin. God saw every sin that we were committed into corrupted shameful desire.

We are fallen in the life that God has given to us. But we were dying in the spirit, soul, and body. Because we were sinners.

If we have to pay our own penalty of our sins and rebel against God, we will truly perish. But God has redeemed us from the curse of the law.

Let's review about what is the curse of the Law. *According to the book of Deuteronomy 28, from verses 15 to 68.*

Start on verse 15 says; **"Curses on Disobedience."** These three things **'suffering of life'** will take place for people:

1. **Spiritual death**
2. **Poverty**
3. **Sickness**

We will find many guidelines and directions from God in Deuteronomy 28.

The Lord has warned them, not to disobey the Lord God of Israel. Disobedience brings a curse upon the people of God.

We read in the Old Covenant, and we praise the Lord that we are living in the New Covenant under His Grace.

And we are free from the curse of the Law. Hallelujah. Amen.

"Christ has redeemed us from the curse of the law, having become a curse for us (for it is written, "Cursed is everyone who hangs on a tree.") Galatians 3:13, NKJV.

Heavy Burden Lifted:

Jesus promised us to give us peace and rest in Him in all situations. Making peace with our fellow men.

Especially giving God's love to others that we can have the fullness of joy.

We must give all our heavy burdens and fear, worry of daily life unto the Lord.

"Come to Me, all you who labor and are heavy laden, and I will give you rest.

Take My yoke upon you and learn from Me, for I am gentle and lowly in heart, and you will find rest for your souls.

For My yoke is easy and My burden is light." Matthew 11:28-30, NKJV.

He Loves Us:

He promised us to love us, and He continues to give us His mercy forever. We cannot compare God's loving heart to anything else in the world.

He never fails to fulfill His promise to Love and care for us. He is our Father in heaven and watches over His children daily.

> **"For the mountains shall depart**
> **And the hills be removed,**
> **But My kindness shall not depart from you,**
> **Nor shall My covenant of peace be removed,**
> **Says the Lord, who has mercy on you."** Isaiah 54:10, NKJV.

He Set Us Free:

God promised us to set us free. We don't allow the devil to deceive us and declare we are not in the slavery of darkness.

We are free indeed. Free from bitterness, unforgiveness, resentment, hatred, covet, and prideful life.

If we're still struggling with temptation, but we are not enslaved to the desire of our will anymore.

> **"Therefore if the Son makes you free, you shall be free indeed."** John 8:36, NKJV.

Believing and Receiving:

God promised us to answer our prayer. In this verse, Jesus says. Have faith in God, and no doubt in our hearts.

The moment we say with our mouth, and with a loud voice. Believing, I have already healed. We say over, over again.

Faith will rise us in our hearts and eventually, we understand, believing the miracles of God belong to us.

If we sincerely believe what we prayed for, then we must receive in his name. This is His will to answer our prayer.

Spending time in His presence to know Him through His Word daily. As the Holy Spirit helps us to understand His Word.

"For assuredly, I say to you, whoever says to this mountain, 'Be removed and be cast into the sea,' and does not doubt in his heart, but believes that those things he says will be done, he will have whatever he says." Mark 11:23, NKJV.

The Prosperity of the Lord:

Biblical **"prosperity"** is not just about wealth, richness, or financial success.

Prosperity is a powerful source of God's blessing from the Lord. It's a plan from God to live a good life of welfare, that consists of economic stability.

It also includes physical health and spiritual happiness. We were also hearing about prosperity, we thought it was all about money and wealth.

But prosperity is about receiving success in every area of our lives.

The Bible states that prosperity is not coming from our own strength but by the authority of God.

The Lord loves to bless us in all areas of life with no sickness and ministry.

There is a verse that will tell us about prospering in all things: what is all things? It means; **everything.**

It can prosper us in good health, finance, knowledge, wisdom, serving others with kindness.

Again, this verse is telling us about receiving good prosperity in **our souls.**

It means; happiness, enjoying life, being cheerful people, living with no fear or worries, and having peace in our hearts.

This is the promise of the Lord to take care of our lives.

"Beloved, I pray that you may prosper in all things and be in health, just as your soul prospers." 3 John 1:2, NKJV.

The Promise of God with Scriptures:

- **The Lord will never leave us or forsake us.**
  "Be strong and of good courage, do not fear nor be afraid of them; for the Lord your God, He is the One who goes with you. He will not leave you nor forsake you." Deuteronomy 31:6, NKJV.
- **The Lord will always strengthen and uphold us.**
  "Fear not, for I am with you;
  Be not dismayed, for I am your God.
  I will strengthen you,
  Yes, I will help you, I will uphold you with My righteous right hand." Isaiah 41:10, NKJV.
- **The Lord will rescue us from every trap and protect us from deadly diseases.**

"Surely He shall deliver you from the snare of the fowler.

And from the perilous pestilence." Psalm 91:3, NKJV.

- **The Lord will go before us and be our rear guard.**

"For you shall not go out with haste,

Nor go by flight;

For the Lord will go before you,

And the God of Israel will be your rear guard." Isaiah 52:12, NKJV.

- **The Lord will fight on our behalf.**

"The Lord will fight for you, and you shall hold your peace." Exodus 14:14, NKJV.

- **The Lord's love will never fail us.**

"For the mountains shall depart.

And the hills be removed,

But *My kindness shall not depart from you,*

Nor shall My covenant of peace be removed,"

Says the Lord, who has mercy on you." Isaiah 54:10, NKJV.

- **The Lord will give His wisdom when we ask Him.**

"If any of you lacks wisdom, let him ask of God, who gives to all liberally and without reproach, and it will be given to him." James 1:5, NKJV.

- **The Lord's plan will prosper us.**
  "For I know the thoughts that I think toward you, says the Lord, thoughts of peace and not of evil, to give you a future and a hope." Jeremiah 29:11, NKJV.

- **God has not given us the spirit of fear.**
  "For God has not given us a spirit of fear, but of power and of love and of a sound mind." 2 Timothy 1:7, NKJV.

- **The Lord will deliver us from all our troubles.**
  "The righteous cry out, and the Lord hears, And delivers them out of all their troubles." Psalm 34:17, NKJV.

- **He comforts us in our time of need.**
  "So we may boldly say: "The Lord is my helper; I will not fear. What can man do to me?" Hebrews 13:6, NKJV.

- **The Lord is our refuge and strong tower in times of trouble.**
  "The Lord also will be a refuge for the oppressed, A refuge in times of trouble." Psalm 9:9, NKJV.

- **The Lord will guide and direct us.**

  "I lay down and slept;

  I awoke, for the Lord sustained me.

  I will not be afraid of ten thousands of people

  Who have set themselves against me all around." Psalm 3:5-6, NKJV.

- **The Lord will bless us and give us the crown of life.**

  "Blessed is the man who endures temptation; for when he has been approved, he will receive the crown of life which the Lord has promised to those who love Him." James 1:12, NKJV.

- **The Lord will give us peace and give us strength.**

  "The Lord gives strength to his people; the Lord blesses his people with peace." Psalm 29:11, NKJV.

- **The Lord will give Grace, Mercy, and Peace.**

  "Grace, mercy, and peace will be with you from God the Father and from the Lord Jesus Christ, the Son of the Father, in truth and love." 2 John 1:3, NKJV.

- **The Lord will make His face shine upon us and be gracious to us.**

"The Lord make His face shine upon you,
And be gracious to you." Numbers 6:25, NKJV.

- **The Lord will give us peace of mind and heart.**

  "Peace I leave with you, My peace I give to you; not as the world gives do I give to you. Let not your heart be troubled, neither let it be afraid." John 14:27, NKJV.

- **The Lord will give the joy of His presence**.

  "You will show me the path of life;
  In Your presence is fullness of joy;
  At Your right hand are pleasures forevermore." Psalm 16:11, NKJV.

- **The Lord will give us a sweet sleep.**

  "When you lie down, you will not be afraid;
  Yes, you will lie down and your sleep will be sweet." Proverbs 3:24, NKJV.

- **The Lord will keep us from all diseases.**

  "And the Lord will take away from you all sickness, and will afflict you with none of the terrible diseases of Egypt which you have known, but will lay them on all those who hate you." Deuteronomy 7:15, NKJV.

- **The Lord will heal us with abundant peace and truth.**

  "Behold, I will bring it health and healing; I will heal them and reveal to them the abundance of peace and truth." Jeremiah 33:6, NKJV.

CHAPTER 6

The Word Never Fails Us

THE WORD OF GOD assures us again that He will never fail us. Jesus is here and standing beside us to strengthen us to victory.

We may not be feeling God's wonderful direction in life. But He has an amazing purpose for our lives.

When we get disheartened, not feel anything about God. We must recognize Him in times of sorrow and sadness.

Sometimes, we think God has left us. At that moment, we take our authority to speak to our discouragement to leave us alone.

God's Word has remained forever and **never ever fails us**. God's truth is perfect for abiding in us, and His Word shall be our shield.

Allow His Word roots in our faith and confidence. Making a great joyful living in God.

Standing Firm:

As we are children of God and needed to stand firm in our faith. God's covenant will never fail in us.

His Word is unbroken, true, pure. He has absolutely established his commitments for our circumstances.

Have you accepted the Lord's promise that He is able to turn around our situation?

He has carried out our problems and His promise is for us to take away every trouble.

Have we proclaimed His praise report for God's glory? Because He will not forsake us from His presence.

Reveal Himself to Us:

God promised to reveal Himself through His Word. We can expect many good things from the Word.

Now many people would ask and seek the Lord. The Bible will make us an understanding to know God in spirit.

The Word can lead us to freedom and relieve unpleasant attitudes. The Holy Spirit will separate us from the disobedience of God.

Inspired by the Spirit of God:

The Scripture itself declares that God's Word is authoritative. We see from the Word that God cannot deceive us.

The Spirit of God has inspired all Scriptures. The Bible is a powerful Word and a dynamic life instruction to all humanity.

God breathes into all His Scriptures. It is useful for **learning, teaching, reproof, and preaching for correction.**

We will use it for instruction in holiness and righteousness. Every believer in Christ may be performing in the spiritual life.

The Holy Spirit will prepare everyone for the excellent work of the ministry. The Word is very alive and active. Amen.

"All Scripture is given by inspiration of God, and is profitable for doctrine, for reproof,

for correction, for instruction in righteousness." 2 Timothy 3:16, NKJV.

God spoken came to Pass:

God's Word is like a seed is planted, and it will produce fruit. It will grow into the spiritual life of everyone who allows to build up inward fruitfulness of life in the Lord.

God's Word is accurate. He assurances us to take care of our everyday life and His wonderworking is excellent.

What God speaks, he will make it happen, he will act on His promise.

We read in the book of Joshua. he declared that every Word that God has spoken came to pass.

"Not a word failed of any good thing which the Lord had spoken to the house of Israel. All came to pass." Joshua 21:45, NKJV.

Staying Calm:

Staying in peace of God is very necessary for every situation. Trust Him in peace of God can be helpful.

Learning all our ways and waiting on the Lord will bring an excellent result. Look at another phrase in verse, **"wait on the Lord."**

This is an excellent encouragement to tell us to wait. We can strengthen ourselves that there are good things and blessings on the way toward us.

I look back on my past, how much mistaken I made. Because I have had a hard time waiting, and I made a quick decision to make a terrible result.

I understood everyone had to act a sudden move in any situation. But the Lord showed up in the place to rescue me.

The Lord Jesus appeared to me and spoke to me, **"why I didn't have any patience to wait on Him."**

Learning is difficult in this kind of situation. When the time arrived to be prepared and He trained me, it was very significant.

I humbled myself under His authority to repent of my mistake to do better. We read another verse to inspire us; it says:

> **"But those who wait on the Lord**
> **Shall renew their strength;**
> **They shall mount up with wings like eagles,**
> **They shall run and not be weary,**

They shall walk and not faint." Isaiah 40:31, NKJV.
Waiting on the Lord:

We see in many scriptures spoke about waiting upon the Lord. Waiting is not an exciting idea for some Christians.

Trusting in the Lord, and He will never delay. In other words, waiting on the Lord means; **"stepping back," "to stand by,"** and rest in the name of the Lord.

We will acknowledge Him to strengthen us as we wait on Him. For some believers, awaiting can be very difficult, and they are not a good situation.

Because when the prayer is done, they expect an answer right away. It is like planting a seed in the ground and waiting for the harvest the next day.

There is a time for everything, a time for prayer, and a time for receiving. Let's look at an encouraging word to stir up our faith.

"Wait on the Lord; Be of good courage, And He shall strengthen your heart; Wait, I say, on the Lord!" Psalm 27:1, NKJV.

Be of Good Courage:

Let's look at another phrase from the verse, **"Be strong."** It would release the spirit of worship to draw us to the presence of the Lord.

Being patient is extremely complicated for everyone. Another phrase in verse, **"take heart and wait for the Lord."**

It shows that we wait for the harvest to arrive and stand firm with a good determination in the Lord.

The more we trust Him and the more to make peace in ourselves. Reading this verse gives us uplifting inspiration in the spiritual life.

This declaration has given to the people of God in the time of Moses.

It really makes us confident that the Lord is watching over us and looking after His children.

"Be strong and of good courage, do not fear nor be afraid of them; for the Lord your God, He is the One who goes with you. He will not leave you nor forsake you." Deuteronomy 31:6, NKJV.

God Moves a big Mountain:

God promised us to move our big mountain. Let's our prayer can be effective and acceptable unto the Lord.

He may move in a situation where no man can get any glory for himself.

I have seen people, along with many Spirit-filled Christians, interceding for each other.

We are finding prayer warriors giving hours and days praying, not giving up.

God has moved mightily, and I had many experiences with how God moved into glory.

As prayer has been answered, hearing the praise report given inspires us. Praying without receiving with no result can bring us down.

But the Spirit of the Lord lifts us up to see more of Him in prayer. I know it is not easy to pray, but faith moves mountains.

He is the God of moving big mountains, and He has done for me. God has even used non-believers to help my situation to solve my problem.

He receives all the glory for Himself. God moves in our worship through tough conditions to bless us and to fulfill His love. Amen.

Nothing is Impossible:

God promised us to help us in an impossible situation. Don't allow every difficulty that will intimidate you.

As I experienced many years of living in the Christian faith. I have gone through the darkest hour of my life.

The Lord has been with me all the time. Then He taught me that I don't need to be afraid of challenges.

He made me strong again. So, as we continue living through the tough times in life.

He is preparing and strengthening us, so we are not terrified of fear.

He is building us up into effective ministers for Himself. He wants us to become mature to the next level of spiritual life.

So, we can achieve the next task for His kingdom. Nothing is hard for the Lord. When we hand over our troubles to the Lord.

He carries out easy ways to make us peace in ourselves and trust in His promise and His power. The Word says,

"Therefore humble yourselves under the mighty hand of God, that He may exalt you in due time, casting all your care upon Him, for He cares for you." 1 Peter 5:6-7, NKJV.

No Weapon Formed Against Us:

The Lord promised us to make courageous men and women become a warrior in daily life. Have we tried to cast out our anxiety on Him?

We get exhausted going through sickness, a financial, and a family crisis. We pray but still do not know what to do.

But if we hold on to our faith in peace and continue to delight ourselves in the Lord.

Then we decree His glorious name shall be manifest, and He is able to make miracles for us. He will appear in the glory of God. Amen.

"No weapon formed against you shall prosper,

And every tongue which rises against you in judgment You shall condemn.

This is the heritage of the servants of the Lord,

And their righteousness is from Me, Says the Lord?" Isaiah 54:17, NKJV.

A Desire to Seek Him:

The Lord promised us to fill us with His presence through prayer and we will find Him.

There is a desire in every human's life to draw himself into prayer and to learn about God. There should be a love for worship to acknowledge Him.

Our love for Jesus takes us near to the Holy Spirit. Let's try to bring ourselves closer to the Word of God.

When we are close, the Holy Spirit will lead us to all knowledge of God. The Word can penetrate the human mind and soul.

Our passion for the Lord should develop to become stronger. Amen.

Believing in His Abilities:

We can take all of His promises not by our works or nor by our human intellectual knowledge.

But we can simply get all His strengths through the grace of God. It requires faith to proclaim His greatness and believe in His abilities.

We will release all His promises from heaven over us. He is reaching out to every area of our lives with the grace and mercy of our God.

If we have tried to control every decision and every area of daily life. Then we think it is not possible to fix it.

But we realize it; there is no way to resolve any crises without the help of the Lord.

Bringing in our mistakes, and we can talk to the Lord in our prayer with honest and humble hearts.

Saying, **"Lord Jesus, I give up, and I will give you all my pride and all my negligence."**

Lord, forgive me, I thought I could fix my problems, but I cannot do it. Lord, I want You to be in authority.

I am exhausted from doing something that is not coming from you. Confess our sins with a loud voice and say to the Lord:

- **Be the Lord of my family.**
- **Be the Lord of my marriage.**
- **Be the Lord of my finances.**
- **Be the Lord of my health.**
- **Be the Lord of my ministry.**

Thank God for His mighty grace and for being in charge of our lives. Amen.

Blessings Confession:

- **I am a child of God.**
  "The Spirit Himself bears witness with our spirit that we are children of God." Romans 8:16, NKJV.

- **I am redeemed from the hand of the enemy.**
  "Let the redeemed of the Lord say *so*, Whom He has redeemed from the hand of the enemy." Psalm 107:2, NKJV.

- **I am saved by grace through faith.**
  "For by grace you have been saved through faith, and that not of yourselves; *it is* the gift of God." Ephesians 2:8, NKJV.

- **I am forgiven of sins.**
  "in whom we have redemption through His blood, the forgiveness of sins." Colossians 1:14, NKJV.

- **I am set free from the law of sin and death.**
  "For the law of the Spirit of life in Christ Jesus has made me free from the law of sin and death." Romans 8:2, NKJV.

- **I am justified by faith.**

  "Therefore, having been justified by faith, we have peace with God through our Lord Jesus Christ." Romans 5:1, NKJV.

- **I am sanctified in the Lord.**

  "And such were some of you. But you were washed, but you were sanctified, but you were justified in the name of the Lord Jesus and by the Spirit of our God." 1 Corinthians 6:11, NKJV.

- **I am a partaker of His divine nature.**

  "by which have been given to us exceedingly great and precious promises, that through these you may be partakers of the divine nature, having escaped the corruption that is in the world through lust." 2 Peter 1:4, NKJV.

- **I am dead to sin but alive in Christ.**

  "Likewise you also, reckon yourselves to be dead indeed to sin, but alive to God in Christ Jesus our Lord." Romans 6:11, NKJV.

- **I am delivered from the power of darkness.**

  "He has delivered us from the power of darkness and conveyed us into the kingdom of the Son of His love." Colossians 1:13, NKJV.

- **I am led by the spirit.**

  "For as many as are led by the Spirit of God, these are sons of God." Romans 8:14, NKJV.

- **I am free from all bondage.**

  "Therefore if the Son makes you free, you shall be free indeed." John 8:36, NKJV.

- **I am protected, wherever I go.**

  "For He shall give His angels charge over you. To keep you in all your ways." Psalm 91:11, NKJV.

- **The Lord will never leave us nor forsake us.**

  "Let your conduct be without covetousness; be content with such things as you have. For He Himself has said, "I will never leave you nor forsake you." Hebrews 13:5, NKJV.

- **I am casting all my cares on Jesus.**

  "casting all your care upon Him, for He cares for you." 1 Peter 5:7, NKJV.

- **I am strong in the Lord and the power of His might.**

  "Finally, my brethren, be strong in the Lord and in the power of His might." Ephesians 6:10, NKJV.

- **I am doing all things through Christ who strengthens me.**

  "I can do all things through Christ who strengthens me." Philippians 4:13, NKJV.

- **I am a hair of God and a join hair with Jesus.**

  "and if children, then heirs—heirs of God and joint heirs with Christ, if indeed we suffer with Him, that we may also be glorified together." Romans 8:17, NKJV.

- **I am hair of the blessings of Abraham.**

  "that the blessing of Abraham might come upon the Gentiles in Christ Jesus, that we might receive the promise of the Spirit through faith." Galatians 3:14, NKJV.

- **I am observing and doing the Lord's commandments.**

  "And the Lord commanded us to observe all these statutes, to fear the Lord our God, for our good always, that He might preserve us alive, as it is this day." Deuteronomy 6:24, NKJV.

- **I am blessed to come in and go out.**

  "Blessed *shall* you *be* when you come in, and blessed *shall* you *be* when you go out." Deuteronomy 28:6, NKJV.

- **I am living everlasting life.**
  "He who believes in the Son has everlasting life; and he who does not believe the Son shall not see life, but the wrath of God abides on him." John 3:36, NKJV.

- **I am alive with Christ and saved by grace.**
  "even when we were dead in trespasses, made us alive together with Christ (by grace you have been saved)." Ephesians 2:5, NKJV.

- **I am healed by His stripes.**
  "who Himself bore our sins in His own body on the tree, that we, having died to sins, might live for righteousness—by whose stripes you were healed." 1 Peters 2:24, NKJV.

- **I am victorious in Christ.**
  "But thanks be to God, who gives us the victory through our Lord Jesus Christ." 1 Corinthians 15:57, NKJV.

- **I am an overcomer by the blood of Lamb and the word of my testimony.**
  "And they overcame him by the blood of the Lamb and by the word of their testimony, and they did not love their lives to the death." Revelation 12:11, NKJV.

- **I am not moved by what I see.**

  "For we walk by faith, not by sight." 2 Corinthians 5:7, NKJV.

- **I am bringing every thought into captivity.**

  "casting down arguments and every high thing that exalts itself against the knowledge of God, bringing every thought into captivity to the obedience of Christ." 2 Corinthians 10:5, NKJV.

- **I am being transformed by the renewing of my mind.**

  "And do not be conformed to this world, but be transformed by the renewing of your mind, that you may prove what is that good and acceptable and perfect will of God." Romans 12:2, NKJV.

- **I am the righteousness of God in Christ.**

  "For He made Him who knew no sin to be sin for us, that we might become the righteousness of God in Him." 2 Corinthians 5:21, NKJV.

- **I am continually praising the Lord with my mouth.**

  "I will bless the Lord at all times; His praise *shall* continually *be* in my mouth." Psalm 34:1, NKJV.

- **I am an imitator of Jesus.**

  "Therefore be imitators of God as dear children." Ephesians 5:1, NKJV.

- **I am rejoicing in the life of Jesus.**

  "And not only that, but we also rejoice in God through our Lord Jesus Christ, through whom we have now received the reconciliation." Romans 5:11, NKJV.

- **I am not controlled by my sinful nature but by the spirit.**

  "But you are not in the flesh but in the Spirit, if indeed the Spirit of God dwells in you. Now if anyone does not have the Spirit of Christ, he is not His." Romans 8:9, NKJV.

- **I am more than a conqueror.**

  "Yet in all these things we are more than conquerors through Him who loved us." Romans 8:37, NKJV.

- **I am victorious.**

  "Now thanks be to God who always leads us in triumph in Christ, and through us diffuses the fragrance of His knowledge in every place." 2 Corinthians 2:14, NKJV.

- **I am strong in my weakness.**

  "Now whom you forgive anything, I also forgive. For if indeed I have forgiven anything, I have forgiven that one for your sakes in the presence of Christ." 2 Corinthians 2:10, NKJV.

- **I am set free from sin.**

  "Stand fast therefore in the liberty by which Christ has made us free, and do not be entangled again with a yoke of bondage." Galatians 5:1, NKJV.

- **I am raised up with Christ and seated with him.**

  "and raised us up together, and made us sit together in the heavenly places in Christ Jesus." Ephesians 2:6, NKJV.

- **I am God's workmanship and masterpiece.**

  "For we are His workmanship, created in Christ Jesus for good works, which God prepared beforehand that we should walk in them." Ephesians 2:10, NKJV.

- **I am justified (declared "not guilty") of sin.**
  "being justified freely by His grace through the redemption that is in Christ Jesus." Romans 3:24, NKJV.
- **I am sanctified (made holy) and acceptable in Christ.**
  "To the church of God which is at Corinth, to those who are sanctified in Christ Jesus, called to be saints, with all who in every place call on the name of Jesus Christ our Lord, both theirs and ours." 1 Corinthians 1:2, NKJV.
- **I am complete in Christ.**
  "and you are complete in Him, who is the head of all principality and power." Colossians 2:10, NKJV.
- **I am not anxious about anything.**
  "Be anxious for nothing, but in everything by prayer and supplication, with thanksgiving, let your requests be made known to God." Philippians 4:6, NKJV.

- **I am always joyful, praying, and giving thanks in all circumstances.**

  "Rejoice always, pray without ceasing, in everything give thanks; for this is the will of God in Christ Jesus for you." 1 Thessalonians 5:16-18, NKJV.

- **I am attentive to the Word of God.**

  "Therefore we must give the more earnest heed to the things we have heard, lest we drift away." Hebrews 2:1, NKJV.

- **I am healed of all sickness and disease in the name of Jesus.**

  "Who forgives all your iniquities, Who heals all your diseases." Psalm 103:3, NKJV.

CHAPTER 7

Prayer of Faith Never Fails

AS WE ARE STUDYING the Word and acknowledging Him that God will never fail to answer our prayer.

If our confidence has failed, we call on the name of Lord Jesus to help us again. His passion never ends, and He doesn't give up on us.

For those of us who have struggled in the spiritual life to not having love to pray. But we can continue to search for Him. He will not neglect us.

Though, what we are experiencing, it might be difficult to ask and trust Him. God sees the prayer of faith.

Discover Him in Prayer:

We will discover more of Him through the Word of God. He has created a prayer to have a living relationship with us.

He is our loving God, as we know God is spirit. So, God wants to have a relationship with us in the spirit.

God has created humans in the spirit, and prayer can make a connection between a man and God.

The Bible says that a human in the spirit must worship God in the spirit and truth. Humans have three parts, body, soul, and spirit.

The spirit of man comes from the One true God. Man cannot survive without the spirit of God.

After the fall of man, he fell into sinful life and death in the spirit of man.

God is love and had compassion over His creation and brought him back into a relationship with Him.

A human can have contact with His creator again. He gave His Son to die on the cross for the entire world.

God gave His love to make intimacy with man through His Son. There is only one way to have an everlasting life with God through Jesus by faith.

Relationship in Prayer:

In the Bible, God has established a relationship between man and Himself through praying and studying the Word of God.

Many people have asked me questions about how they can find God through prayer.

For example, they ask, **"Who is God? How can we find Him? Does God exist?"**

Many questions will be answered in this book; I will explain them from topic to topic.

Let's look at how God made a connection possible for us as we may go into His presence through His Son.

God has designed many forms of prayer to have a relationship with Him in unique ways:

- **The prayer of thanksgiving would come along with praise and worship.**
- **The prayer of faith carries out a petition to ask God with a unique outcome.**

- **The prayer of agreement brings two or three to come together in one accord.**
- **The prayer of intercession is standing in the gap on behalf of someone else.**
- **The prayer of consecration is making a dedication to the work of the Lord.**

Needed the Anointing:

Why do we need anointing in our prayer? Because we need the empowerment of the Fire of God for our spiritual life and our own ministry.

As we experienced, the Holy Spirit is more powerful than any other spirit in the world. By the help of the Spirit would bring victory from all negative thoughts.

We believe He is the Anointed One, to care for us and break all shackles of darkness and sickness in our lives.

We need anointing in our prayer to show us direction: How to pray! He teaches us to learn from Him to walk in triumph.

We will overcome any attack of the enemy, and we shall break off in His name. Amen.

Jesus Fights for Us:

When we pray with persistent desire, the Lord will not leave us. He will stand with us, and He fights a good fight for us.

He is taking us to a high level of understanding that our Lord is a victorious God. He brings us answers to everyone's prayers.

If we have the right mindset, persistent prayer sets our hearts upon the Word. It leads us to move forward to follow His plan.

He is able to change everything to bring great joy to us. We testify that He is making a difference in our situation.

Not To Be a Quitter:

When we look back at our own early Christian walk with the Lord. We realize we made many mistakes in the past.

But we desired to run back to the Lord and make ourselves right with Him. Being a persistent prayer would bring us delight.

It is so good to press on for a long time and call for His grace. I always loved seeking Him for His Will to be done in my life.

We all go through disaster experiences. But our Lord is the God of second chances, and if we don't give up very easily.

He will lead us into a mighty triumph at the right time for us. We must have this kind of attitude to be cheerful in our hearts.

Get ready to grow into prayer warriors and look forward to receiving victory in prayer. He is releasing answers from heaven to us. To God, be the glory.

The Story of a Widow:

Persistent prayer is coming from the Word of God. It reminds me of the enjoyable story of a widow.

Probably, you have heard it many times. But it is written in the book of Luke, chapter 18.

There was a widow who lived in the town, and she had a big problem with the law. She heard about a judge who was working in court.

She said to herself. I will go to ask this judge in the town. It might be he can help me out with my trouble.

She decided to appear in front of a judge for sympathy. So, she went there to meet the judge, but he didn't care for her needs.

She was pleading for justice and requesting her case to be granted. For a long time, she was knocking at the door of a judge for mercy.

She was expecting and waiting to receive the blessing. Because of her pray and seeking more, and her mindset was not to give up.

She didn't quit but pressed for more. The judge saw her and heard about her problems.

Finally, the judge said to himself, this woman is pleading for justice all the time, and she is wearing me out.

"I need to grant her mercy." The judge gave her petition.

"Now there was a widow in that city; and she came to him, saying, 'Get justice for me from my adversary.'

And he would not for a while; but afterward he said within himself, 'Though I do not fear God nor regard man, yet because this widow troubles me I will avenge her, lest by her continual coming she weary me.'" Luke 18:3-5, NKJV.

His Voice in Prayer:

The Holy Spirit speaks to me in prayer; He trained me to hear His voice.

We must recognize the authority of God to prepare our spirit for the next level of wisdom and knowledge.

The Spirit of God loves to teach us confidence and has a gentle voice. When He speaks to us or sometimes whispers in our spiritual ears.

He is very kind, and He is a loving person. The Holy Spirit is disciplining us in our prayer to trust and not have any doubt.

Let's read these verses, and it will inspire us as well.

"Trust in the Lord with all your heart,
And lean not on your own understanding;
In all your ways acknowledge Him,
And He shall direct your paths." Proverbs 3:5-6, NKJV.

Empower Us in Prayer:

Sometimes we cannot pray because of the heavy burden in our spirit. If we ask Him, He empowers us to conquer and reveals to us what lacks in our prayer life.

By the power of His anointing, He is fighting to remove all our confusion. He makes us ready to renew our minds and restore our spirit.

Make yourself available for more powerful prayer time again. Are we asking ourselves sometimes why our prayer life is dried?

We need more anointing to go up into a higher power to pray in the spirit. Yes, it is becoming obvious to see what it lacks in prayer.

The Holy Spirit is saying to us when we feel there is no power in our prayer life. We assume it is very dry, and we don't enjoy our prayer time.

It is a moment when we should ask the Holy Spirit to fill us with more of **His dynamic anointing.**

He knows how to pour out a fresh spirit in us and baptize us with His power. He loves to change us into mighty men and women of prayer. Amen.

Fear Must Go:

We all have the spirit of fear, no matter who we are; it is a part of human nature.

The Word of God teaches an understanding of anxiety and worries and how to overcome these spirits.

We must remember, these doubts, restlessness, and worries are spirits.

We can acknowledge them and command all spirits of fear to come out of our prayer time.

Our spiritual authority should cancel all their plans and destruction.

Remember, we have all the spiritual authority that Jesus has given to us to rebuke the devil.

He gave us a mighty power to overcome all false spirits with his accusations and more.

A Strong Believer:

When the prayer of faith starts in our hearts, our spirit builds up the courage. It tells us: **"I am in the right place, and I am a strong believer in my faith."**

Wherever I go, the Lord is with me; He is surrounding us with His favor.

It is a sign of Christian maturity to believe no one can separate us from the presence of the Lord.

We should continuously be calling on the Holy Spirit, who is always ready to lead us and guide us in the right direction.

He is speaking to us all the time through many different situations.

Casting out Doubt:

We can get rid of every spirit of fear casting them out by the power of our words. If we don't cast out these spirits, it will bring more crises and lose our peace.

Try again to speak out of every doubt, fear, and worry. Speak aloud to those spirits' names by name, telling them to come out of your life.

When the moment, the Lord would set you free from these spirits.

You start to worship the Lord with powerful praise music to build up your spirit to be in His presence.

We can then continue living with a clean and humble heart before the Lord.

If we make a mistake to bring back all fears, worries, and doubts again.

It may happen those fears will come back with more spirits to our lives in the future.

We must speak boldly to all fears to go out. We can cast out them in our lives. Amen.

Rejoice in Him:

We need to move forward to get our joy back. Let's our praise and worship would bring down the Fire of God.

We are entering into the presence of the Lord with peace. Rejoicing in the Lord is extremely effective and having comfort in prayer.

We all expect an answer from the Lord with enjoyment. We rejoice in prayer because we depend on His Word.

We trust in His presence and His spirit. He is alive and is here with us. We are not alone by ourselves.

He is anointing us to rejoice in His salvation and His love. He is dealing with all problems and resolving our chaos at work or in the family. Amen.

CHAPTER 8

Surrendering to God's Plan

SURRENDERING TO GOD'S PLAN is the best way of submitting everything in His Will.

Whatever the Lord has laid in our hearts, we will do it to the best of our capability.

God rewards honest men and women of God to be obedient to His plan. He will bless faithful, humble servants.

We will do the work of the Kingdom with excellence, honor, honesty, love, kindness, and goodwill.

We are obeying all good work for sake of His Kingdom. When we perform it with the help of the Lord?

He will anoint us with the fresh Fire of His presence from heaven.

Yielding to His Plan:

Learning to yield everything in God's plan. It's the greatest pathway to happiness.

Because the purpose of God is perfect, and he wants us to be a part of his plan.

We must have the heart to surrender what God desires to do in our lives. So, usually, we have determined in all our ways by ourselves.

God requires doing the work of miracles in our lives to heal us and grow us up. He is seeing from the starting point to the end.

He has a very better plan for our lives than we make. True submission is not only the surrender of our external way of life.

But when we're handing over our desire, our will, and then our surrender will be made under His Word.

The greatest trouble we constantly deal with is the yielding of our hearts.

Even though, God never forces a person's life to submit himself to the Will of God.

He quietly waits until every individual believer voluntarily returns to the Lord.

We Surrender unto Jesus:

I experience in my own prayer time when I really desired to push forward to get my prayer to succeed. I feel that I want to have an answer right away.

I struggle to show myself to be in charge of prayer. Thank God I am not that kind of person in demand of my prayer anymore.

I learned that I must allow Him to be in charge of all my troubles and problems.

He should be in control and lead my prayer by the Holy Spirit.

You have probably heard this phrase, **"Let Jesus do it."** Because the Lord Jesus is doing a marvelous job for us.

Let Jesus controls your family and your children, allow Him to be in charge of your finances.

In fact, many people are telling me, "I cannot manage my money and my businesses."

We say, **"Lord Jesus, You can have all of these things."** Lord, You can manage correctly for me.

"Teach us to become wiser in all areas," He makes us smarter on how to make the right decision daily.

Recognize Him to take control over you. Tell Him these words.

"Lord, I am 'authorizing' You to take control of everything that you have given to me."

Seven Declarations of God's power:

Lord, You are the one to be in charge of my life, my family, my job, my ministry, and my finances.

Learning to let go of our own control in prayer. Surrendering to the hand of the Almighty God, then He turns into great blessings.

Committing our personal Christian walk with Him will be enjoyable. That reminded me of the book of Revelation, where it says:

"Worthy is the Lamb who was slain, to receive power and riches and wisdom. And strength and honor and glory and blessing!" Revelation 5:12, NKJV.

These Words are the promises, and we have all seven declarations of God's power. We claim it for our own lives.

These declarations are; **Power, Riches, Wisdom, Strength, Honor, Glory, Blessings.**

We declare all seven blessings from the book of Revelation are ours. Amen.

Committing our Desire into God's Will:

We must lean on Jesus and let go of whatever is holding us back for not experiencing His grace.

God's loving-kindness and purpose are far higher than anything in the world. He sees better than we achieve in every situation.

He knows every detail of our way of life and let's allow ourselves to go under His authority.

He doesn't leave us alone with no purpose of His plan. When we submit to our will into His Will, He gives us peace and uses us for His Glory.

Depend on God:

Handing over all our ideas and passions to serve God. We're moving forward by faith in His Words and trust in His promises.

We can step out into freedom from doubts and fear of the future. Remember, He is able to transform us into magnificent men and women of God.

He wants us to declare His Words to perform His sovereignty. We really must be determined to depend on God for everything.

If we can count on God for our Salvation and redemption through Jesus. We can have also hoped in Him for our everyday needs and ambitions.

Practicing our Surrender:

Practicing our surrender is a daily routine, by our humble heart, to make the right choice.

It's just like in every change in the way of spiritual life. We must determine to surrender and hand over to the Lord.

Obey His Words to become easier when we are ready to study and to understand His plan.

The enemy is trying to bring negative thoughts in every believer.

If we allow the devil to control our minds and he creates more worries with fears and doubts.

The devil wishes more crises were effectively thrown into our lives. Yielding everything under God's authority.

Learning in a daily habit of turning all our problems to Jesus and He cares for us.

Surrender Negative Thoughts:

Whenever any negative thoughts undertake to penetrate our minds. We know what to do; we must decree the Word to all attack of the enemy.

We can cut them off and give our minds to the Lord to refresh us again.

God's graces are fresh every day, and we don't pay any attention to past experiences.

So, what it takes place, the joy of the Lord is completely residing in us again. Carrying the old memory will not help us.

In fact, to take us in the wrong direction toward enemy territory and he will rob our peace from us. God's mercy and grace are following us all the days of our lives.

Take the Word into our hearts to meditate and claim our victory, then renew our minds in Christ. Amen.

Surrendering a Good Character:

A true Christian believer should have a willing spirit to obey in submission. Living with humility to surrender is an excellent character of prayer.

Having an attitude of yielding all things in the presence of the Lord.

We read many marvelous stories in the New Testament. Stephen had an obedient heart.

"And Stephen, full of faith and power, did great wonders and signs among the people." Acts 6:8, NKJV.

He had a powerful faith to please the Lord; he was ready to give himself up and be stoned.

We recognize that many apostles were very obedient to their faith.

But they didn't give up, and they didn't yield their faith to other gods. In fact, they were Christian martyrs for the sake of the Lord.

They gathered in one place to pray for protection and guidance for what would come next. We learn from these brave disciples and all apostles of the Lord.

Standing in the difficult time:

Those early churches were living in challenging times. They had a lot of persecutions, but they continued serving and preaching the Word of God.

We must learn how to abide in Him in all circumstances of our Christian life. We are staying strong to steadfast in dark times and happy times.

When the times of adversity would take place, we're standing on the Word.

"Now he who keeps His commandments abides in Him, and He in him.

And by this we know that He abides in us, by the Spirit whom He has given us." 1 John 3:24, NKJV.

Learning to yield to His Word and knowing the plan and the anointing of God.

Let's surrender to His power, give ourselves under His protection, and to His glory.

To become easy to submit under His will, when He speaks to us.

Sometimes we get confused and ask Jesus a lot of questions like, why do I need to do this? For example:

Lord, if I don't get along with this person? Do I need to pray for that person?

Questions will be there in our minds all the time. But He has the answer for everything.

Yield and Obey His Word:

When we start hearing Him, then we go to minister to someone inside or outside of the church.

We must live on fire of the Holy Spirit to yield and to be obedient to His Word.

God makes surprises for us, and we see people get freed and transformed.

I especially love to pray for healing. I am always ready to give a prophetic word and prayer for restoration.

The Lord tells me to pray for that person with their family. I began to pray for their sick body.

If the Lord tells me to pray for a person along with their loved one, I am willing to intercede in prayer.

I am continually ready to obey the Lord and to hear how He wants me to pray for healing's recovery.

Allowing Him to Control Us:

Usually, we want to control everything in any situation in our daily life.

Managing and controlling are the toughest thing to give up, then we feel weak.

Spiritual maturity will help us to understand the concept of going under the authority of God. He is already handling our conditions.

We need to allow His power to change us. Let Him lead us by His Holy Spirit to teach His Way.

He is the maker of the universe, so we can depend on Him in daily life.

Learning His ability from His Words that He is always faithful to His Words.

Speak life with our mouth and change our mindset to the good things of God. Amen.

Surrender our Worries:

It is a natural reaction for every human and Christian believer to get worried.

If we go through a rough time and are afraid of everything in our daily activities.

As God's Word said, worry will not add a single day to our lives. In fact, fear, worry, doubt would paralyze us and make us unfunctional nature every day.

Worry can truly influence us not entirely our minds, souls, bodies and but our spirits will lose peace of God.

Being anguish produces really nothing good. Surrender our concern to the Lord and He is taking care of our lives.

"Be anxious for nothing, but in everything by prayer and supplication, with thanksgiving, let your requests be made known to God." Philippians 4:6, NKJV.

Be Guided by Prayer:

God requires us to guide our lives and our decision-making by reading His Words daily. He declares such advice in His Word.

"I will instruct you and teach you in the way you should go; I will guide you with My eye." Psalms 32:8, NKJV.

Therefore, everyone who seeks to do smart decisions and experience God's will must always ask for instruction.

As we pray, and we will search for His leadership in which He is directing us to an important task.

Asking Him for guidance and He will take us to a powerful life of wisdom, purity, and bravery.

"You are my rock and my fortress; Therefore, for Your name's sake, Lead me and guide me." Psalms 31:3, NKJV.

Committing our Relationship:

I mean, our relationship with the Lord is reflecting our love for people around us.

It will be enjoyable serving and God's love will flow into everyone's heart.

The Lord will expect us to serve others with a humble spirit. Submitting our willingness to hand of God, then He will use us for His plan.

Sometimes we have difficulty laying down our pride to minister to needy people.

Being guided by the Holy Spirit to get more anointing to witness the Gospel to those who have not heard the Good News.

Jesus died for everyone because He loves us, and He cares for all of us. The Lord has given us authority to share the Good News of Love of God.

Let's use our message of the Gospel to our families and friends. They need the salvation of God. Amen.

Our future is in God's Plan:

Living one day at a time, we cannot add any day or add any day from yesterday.

Learning to live the joy of the Lord, not allowing any situation to rob our peace and joy.

Speaking to ourselves when we recognize that our Lord is in control of our daily lives.

Giving up ourselves into God's hands and trust in our hearts that we are protected by His Glory.

It is true, each day is a gift from God! We must train our minds how to surrender everything to Him and trust Him, even we don't understand it?

When our minds become occupied with all strange thoughts. We can count on God in our future.

We try to manage and make a plan for the future, but the Lord has a wonderful plan to bless us. Seeking our fulfillment in life today will satisfy us. Amen.

Struggles to Surrender:

Let's go to the Lord and express ourselves with thanksgiving and praise unto Him.

If there are a lot of struggles with our surrender because we don't know how to submit ourselves under His authority.

It becomes very easy to confess our weakness to Him, and the Holy Spirit will lead us in the right direction.

He wants us to lay down all our problems, sins, sickness, and unknowing things in our lives.

He knows every area that we are fighting and not having victory over it. Call unto the Lord for help and trust in Him seriously.

Handing over our daily battles into His presence in prayer. Tell Him **"Lord, Your will be done in my life."**

We must declare God's supremacy over everything. Through worship, thanksgiving, prayer; we will receive how to submit our plan to God totally. Amen.

Surrendering to God's Will:

Knowing God's will and recognizing Him to His good work, then training ourselves in the Word.

We must decide to let go of whatever is keeping us back from experiencing His lovingkindness.

God's direction and strategy are much better than everything we can imagine.

He sees more than we achieve and knows every uncovering thing of our lives.

He is with us and for us who can be against us every day. When we leave an impossible situation to lay down on the Alter under His power.

He leads us in peace that establishes our hearts with the joy of the Lord.

He makes our souls rest because we proclaim by our mouth, we trust in His will. He is our victory.

The enemy doesn't like it to declare the name of Jesus when we seek the Lord.

The enemy is trying to control our circumstances for us without God.

When tough moments fall into our lives. We hold fast in our belief by our own faith to fight a good fight of faith.

But we know without the Word of God we can do nothing. Remember, speaking and declaring the Word in the right situation will give a glorious victory.

The Word will never fail us. The Word always works wonderfully for the Glory of God.

However, the further we do by ourselves to control the results of prayer. It literally creates us less receiving.

Because we must decree the Word is our authority in all situations. God in His mercy is watching us over everywhere.

He is waiting to teach us a great way to victory. In Jesus' name. Amen.

CHAPTER 9

Declaring God's Word

THE WORD OF GOD is the foundation of our faith and believing in God that He exists.

Declaring God's Word is the manifestation of our faith and believing the Word is truth.

Believing in God's Word is the core of our faith. Claiming the Word with our mouth gives the power of faith into action.

Declare means: *Formally announce, to proclaim, to inform, to the decree, and authorize to manifest.*

There is a biblical declaration that can be revealed about God having spoken with the Word.

As a believer to speaking out of our mouth is extremely vital. He establishes His Word with the truth, and we stand firm on what we believe.

Let's set up our hearts by studying the Word, then the Spirit of God reveals a new revelation to us.

We see clearly indicate what God has declared to create something out of nothing.

Power in our Tongues:

There is a power in our tongues in every human being. It means our words have power.

In fact, the Word said: **Death and life in the power of our tongue.**

In the book of James said: A tongue is like a rudder is a technique used to steer a boat, airplane, ship...

As just a rudder controls the way of a ship, and our words affect the control of our lives.

"Death and life are in the power of the tongue, And those who love it will eat its fruit." Proverbs 18:21, NKJV.

We need to proclaim God's Word over our lives that it shall be established for us.

If we speak a positive word, we receive good things. *If we speak negatively, we receive a negative harvest.*

Then we experience a life of blessing with peace and happiness with good health.

Layout a few outlines of scriptures to claim God's Word daily for our lives. We have the promise of His Words to perform miracles.

He has watched over us by His presence. His Word said: He is ready to perform it when we ask Him.

The Word of the Lord is ready to declare His Glory and bring an answer from heaven. Faith brings His words into reality.

God's Word will never fail anyone who seeks Him diligently. He will accomplish what He said in His Word. Amen.

Affirming God's promises:

Affirming God's promises with a spirit of mistrust prevents us from not receiving anything.

But if we decree our words, and align with His Words, we will receive more of Him.

If we are new believers in the Lord Jesus, we can be passionate about practicing the promise of God.

First, we must acknowledge His Word in all circumstances that He is able to do miracles.

Second: His Word will always make it possible for us to believe in Him through our faith.

Third: His Words cannot fail anyone who believes and declares His mighty authority.

Once we're settled, to know the authority of speaking, believing, and agreeing with God's truth.

We are ready to claim His words over our situations as new believers.

Declaration for Daily Life:

In everyday life, we are making many choices by saying the right words and wrong words.

Even though we don't pay any attention to our conversation with others.

Every word will come out of our mouth and we cannot put those words back into our mouth again.

Many times, we pick up a lot of different words from our hearts.

Maybe we don't want to say at the right time or the right place. It will affect our daily choices and change our blessings.

We can choose to listen to other opinions of men, and we can choose to declare our belief in the Word of God.

We can be determined to acknowledge God's Word and stand on the Word.

The decision is ours and does not involve us in any conflict with anyone else.

Declaring with Boldness:

I genuinely believe the Lord chooses us to be dynamic in every aspect of His Kingdom.

He wishes us to seek Him and to depend on Him only. Standing on the Word, especially on His promises.

I think it is an honor to walk on fire of the Holy Spirit. I advise making an effective prayer to speak up, praying a little bit loud, and not being a shy person in public.

I remember what the Holy Spirit reveals to me if I pray loud, going with the flow of the Holy Spirit.

Actually, I preach loudly in the air and teach the Word to the people around me.

In fact, I pray to break off every yoke and tear down a chain of bondages.

I love to seek God by preaching to myself. So, I go ahead to declare with a strong voice, and the devil doesn't like it.

But the Holy Spirit is leading me into a dream and vision for my future ministry.

The Fire of God is leading us to victory from ordinary to extraordinary. Amen.

Speak 'Life' into Our Conditions:

Scriptures are filled with truths of God's Word that confirm the authority of our tongues.

The Word gave us a strong anointing, which the Lord has poured out inside of us.

The favor of God has been released over us because we're living in Him.

No negative word can be helpful to our situations. Even our problems go down more than makes it better.

Because of our lack of knowledge, we bring our blessings down; we speak up many negatives spoken words.

There is an anointing and power, **the favor of God is sitting there and waiting for us to possess them.**

But we tear them down, because of **a misunderstanding of our own mistakes.**

Although we need to change our attitude and behavior toward our situations.

The Holy Spirit has already anointed us with fresh oil every day.

A fresh oil a symbolic of the Holy Spirit and our desire to receive God's blessings.

Even though we don't see anything with our physical eyes. But the result of spoken words brings Life to our healing in our sickness.

Persistent spoken Word of God will never fail us. Continue preaching to our sickness; say over and over in a loud voice. **"I believe, I receive my healing."**

Miracles shall happen from our spoken word to create Life for our diseases.

This is faith makes a difference to every word that we speak with a loud voice.

I speak Life into my healing and miracles. Do not have any doubt and believe that He is able to perform His wonders. In Jesus's name. Amen.

The Whole Arm of God:

Proclaiming God's word creates faith to align our spirits with God's Word. When we say his Word, his truthfulness builds inside of us.

Then we set up our desire to agree with His Will. The Word is encouraging us to put on the whole armor of God.

Taking the helmet of salvation. Having the sword of the Spirit, which is the word of God.

"And take the helmet of salvation, and the sword of the Spirit, which is the word of God." Ephesians 6:17, NKJV.

When Jesus begins fasting for 40 days and was tempted in the wilderness by Satan. He said to him by God's Word only, and he left Him alone.

Claiming God's word allows us to have more victory through temptations and trials of life.

As a believer in the Lord, we have the power to overcome every situation that will come against us.

The Word has power, living and active. Because the Spirit of Living of God lives in the Word.

We must have confidence in our faith that there is an authority in the Word of God.

The Bible will assure us of new life to make us full confident.

We really desire to be strong by accepting His blessings and saying those words over our lives. Amen.

Miracles Come Forward:

The Lord gives us spiritual understanding with a new thought. He will strengthen us to speak from an impossible situation into existence.

Then we will build up our faith in His plan to fulfill our destiny. He chooses us to make us mature in His knowledge, authority, and miraculous strength.

So that we can carry the Gospel to unsaved people to be the witness of His Glory.

Serving Him in His kingdom is very honorable. His miracle is already here in our midst, and it's become reality to us.

But it is up to us to receive them and to recognize the revelation of God. Our hearts will call them out to come forward. Amen.

Positive Confession:

Acknowledging the word of God is one form of triumph wc can conquer over every spirit.

Confessing the truth and promise of God in prayer will transform our circumstances.

We can say these confessions as we have devotion in prayer in the morning and evening.

Praying these scriptures with a loud voice will be used in the spirit realm.

We speak the Word is **'the Life'** will go into the atmosphere to fulfill our destiny.

Finding the scriptures in the Bible to promise us to fulfill our situations and conditions come to pass.

Let's read and study the scriptures. If we choose to experience these positive confessions.

We must be eager to do our part and wait on the Lord to bring His blessings.

Positive confession will bring joy, hope, and peace to our lives.

We speak out His truth and we're a partner with God's word as we shout out his truthfulness.

Positive statements are accomplished by our Christian faith. God's desire is for us to have His benefits, healing, and miracles.

We will have a fresh anointing to do His Will and receive all His passion and love. Amen.

"This Book of the Law shall not depart from your mouth, but you shall meditate in it day and night, that you may observe to do according to all that is written in it. For then you will make your way prosperous, and then you will have good success." Joshua 1:8, NKJV.

Speaking a Right Word:

The Lord is teaching in His Word concerning our **'speak'** should be good in the way we talk every day.

There is a verse in the book of Proverbs that would say: **we must be very careful, what words will come out of our mouth.**

The Word is saying, **get rid of a deceitful mouth from a wrongful heart and it will take us on the wrong path.**

The Lord is expecting us to talk a good talk but not have a perverse mouth. I think we will be accountable for our actions.

He wants us to declare a true confession of faith to speak up **'Praise Report'** of the Lord.

Being a wise Christian believer to declare a pleasant word come out of our mouth to glorify Jesus. Amen.

"Put away from you a deceitful mouth,

And put perverse lips far from you." Proverbs 4:24, NKJV.

Declaration of His Creation:

God has created all things for His pleasure that He may establish His throne.

The heavens will proclaim God's sovereignty, His glory and we recognize God's supremacy.

There will be a declaration of God's will, His plan, and His promises for our salvation.

We must decree His Word by faith and not say other things which are not aligned with God's Word.

When He created us in His image, He wanted to reach out to us through His Word. He chooses to reveal His plan to us and decree all His promises.

As we believe that He promised us to save the whole world by sending His Son Jesus for us.

God has revealed Himself to us with glorious revelations alone in His Word. We believe that His Word is the living Scriptures.

God's authoritative power to make a loving relationship with His people.

God's desire for us to have all good things by declaring His blessings will come to pass. Amen.

Believing and Declaring:

There is a power of speaking a word with our bold faith to unlock our destiny.

Sometimes we miss proclaiming the faithfulness of His Goodness and especially His love toward us.

As long as we are experiencing His miracles and healing in our bodies. He is here to deliver us and help in our time of need.

As we see, the Holy Spirit is here in the midst of us everywhere. He has established our lives for His own Glory.

We belong to Him. All things come from His Words, His plan, His will, and His promises given to us.

Our faith begins declaring God's Word over our lives, our family, our career, our health, our finance, and our ministry.

Confession of our faith will bless us and receive a fresh experience of His Life and blessing. Amen.

Stand Strong to Decree:

We stand strong to decree what is right for our lives and what the Word says.

Every Word in the Bible is true and there is no error in the Word. I claim to accept God's Word.

Surrendering ourselves along with a good Christian friend will bring blessings to our lives.

Let's each day we make the declaration from the Word which has promised to us.

Start our day by claiming them by faith and then declaring them throughout the day.

As we repeat these proclamations, our needs for healing, prayer request for miracles, our dreams, and our visions.

They shall be established by our spoken words in our lives. In Jesus' name. Amen.

- **I declare:** I am a child of God.
  "The Spirit Himself bears witness with our spirit that we are children of God." Romans 8:16, NKJV.

- **I declare:** I am forgiven.

  "If we confess our sins, He is faithful and just to forgive us our sins and to cleanse us from all unrighteousness." 1 John 1:9, NKJV.

- **I declare:** I have no fear, guilt, or condemnation in my life.

  "In Him we have redemption through His blood, the forgiveness of sins, according to the riches of His grace." Ephesians 1:7, NKJV.

- **I declare:** I will serve the Lord.

  "Serve the Lord with gladness; Come before His presence with singing." Psalm 100:2, NKJV.

- **I declare:** I am not weary to achieve the good things.

  "And let us not grow weary while doing good, for in due season we shall reap if we do not lose heart." Galatians 6:9, NKJV.

- **I declare:** I hear God's voice, He is my Good shepherd.

  "And when he brings out his own sheep, he goes before them; and the sheep follow him, for they know his voice." John 10:4, NKJV.

- **I declare:** The goodness and mercy of God shall follow me every day.

  "Surely goodness and mercy shall follow me, All the days of my life; And I will dwell in the house of the Lord Forever." Psalms 23:6, NKJV.

- **I declare:** The favor of God is with me and having favor with God and with man. **"And so find favor and high esteem. In the sight of God and man."** Proverbs 3:4, NKJV.

- **I declare:** My vision is come to pass.

  "For the vision is yet for an appointed time; But at the end it will speak, and it will not lie. Though it tarries, wait for it; Because it will surely come, It will not tarry." Habakkuk 2:3, NKJV.

- **I declare:** God's favor will surrender me *as with a shield.*

  "For You, O Lord, will bless the righteous; With favor You will surround him as with a shield." Psalm 5:12, NKJV.

- **I declare:** God is pouring out His blessing and opening the windows of heaven over my life.

  "Bring all the tithes into the storehouse, That there may be food in My house,

And try Me now in this, "Says the Lord of hosts,"

If I will not open for you the windows of heaven.

And pour out for you such blessing.

That there will not be room enough to receive it." Malachi 3:10, NKJV.

- **I declare:** I am a peacemaker, and I have the fullness of peace in my life.

  "Blessed are the peacemakers,

  For they shall be called sons of God." Matthew 5:9, NKJV.

- **I declare:** I am fearfully and wonderfully made.

  "I will praise You, for I am fearfully and wonderfully made;

  Marvelous are Your works,

  And that my soul knows very well." Psalm 139:14, NKJV.

- **I declare:** I am alive because Jesus lives in me.

  "I have been crucified with Christ; it is no longer I who live, but Christ lives in me; and the life which I now live in the flesh I live by faith in the Son of God, who loved me and gave Himself for me." Galatians 2:20, NKJV.

- **I declare:** I love Jesus because He loved me first.

  "We love Him because He first loved us." 1 John 4:19, NKJV.

- **I declare:** I am fulness of His wisdom and understanding with the peace of God. **"But the wisdom that is from above is first pure, then peaceable, gentle, willing to yield, full of mercy and good fruits, without partiality and without hypocrisy."** James 3:17, NKJV.

- **I declare:** I receive supernatural strength, and my angels are carrying out the Word to me while I speak.

  "Bless the Lord, you His angels,
  Who excel in strength, who do His word,
  Heeding the voice of His word." Psalm 103:20, NKJV.

- **I declare:** I bring every thought into captivity to the obedience of Christ.

  "For the weapons of our warfare are not carnal but mighty in God for pulling down strongholds, casting down arguments and every high thing that exalts itself against the knowledge of God, bringing every thought

into captivity to the obedience of Christ." 2 Corinthians 10:4-5, NKJV.

- **I declare:** I am the head and not the tail, I shall be above only, and not be beneath.

  "And the Lord will make you the head and not the tail; you shall be above only, and not be beneath, if you heed the commandments of the Lord your God, which I command you today, and are careful to observe them." Deuteronomy 28:13, NKJV.

- **I declare:** I am taking back what the enemy has stolen from me to be restored.

  "Yet when he is found, he must restore sevenfold; He may have to give up all the substance of his house." Proverbs 6:31, NKJV.

CHAPTER 10

New Seasons of Growth

WE CAN FIND A phrase in the Bible. It says there will be a season of sowing a seed and reaping a harvest.

In order to understand God's timing throughout many seasons of life. We must see to distinguish between **'sowing' and 'receiving.'**

As a believer, we acknowledge the true authority of God throughout the Bible.

God performs his will in every human's life in his own perfect time.

Understanding to agree with God's Word is fundamental to getting freedom from the pains of suffering.

Surrendering our daily tasks to God's true timing is to know Him better. He wants us to know His marvelous wonders every day.

His Word is powerful, and He is in control of time. He made a Time for us on the earth.

> **"While the earth remains,**
> **Seedtime and harvest,**
> **Cold and heat,**
> **Winter and summer,**
> **And day and night,**
> **Shall not cease."** Genesis 8:22, NKJV.

Spiritual Growth:

Spiritual growth is the transformation process of becoming more like Jesus.

When we put our confidence in the Lord, the Holy Spirit leads and prepares us like Him.

He is making us into His image. God's power is established into our divine destiny.

It says we have **"everything we need"** in His Holy Word for living abounding life.

Living of godliness, which is the purpose of spiritual growth in Christian life.

What we desire to develop our knowledge of Him. **It means winning everything in the life of His victory.**

He poured out His Holy Spirit to equip us for our lives' growth. Amen.

Becoming Like Jesus:

There is a process of spiritual growth to becoming more mature in the Lord. When we are in one's relationship with Him.

Nothing matters to us, what is going around us. As long as we are in the right fellowship in His presence by reading His Word, that's important for us.

Being close to Him every day, and our personal relationship become stronger.

We're growing spiritually, and we're walking in the Light of Jesus, becoming more and more like Christ.

Spiritual maturity is very important for us, to make us sensitive to the spirit of darkness.

I mean, we will be able to **"identify good from evil."** The Spirit of God is alive and ready to come into our lives.

Any time we give our hearts to the Lord Jesus, the Holy Spirit will come dwelling in us.

Spiritual growth starts the time we accept Christ by faith. We should continue living a victorious life.

We enter into the presence of Christ by reading His Word, declaring His promises, and testifying His name.

"But solid food belongs to those who are of full age, that is, those who by reason of use have their senses exercised to discern both good and evil." Hebrews 5:14, NKJV.

Changing to a New Season:

We are experiencing every new season which is taking us to a fresh miracle.

The Lord brings our lives to change for good with His kindnesses.

He challenges us to learn about our spiritual growth to be a witness of His Glory.

Just as we go through the weather experiences various seasons.

No one can move the work of nature, at the same time one season will work in God's direction.

So, the times of our spiritual lives must be changed to become stronger as well.

Knowing what spiritual season, we are? From a new believer to a mature believer and growing of our faith.

The source of our faith must be in the Word alone and believing in His marvelous power.

The Lord wants to have a relationship with us to make us a warrior. Spiritual growth is a way of new life to experience Jesus in truth.

It is also a commitment to walk by faith, not by feeling. When we know the Word and recognize Jesus as Lord, Savior, a healer, and as a miracle worker.

The purpose of spiritual transformation is to become like Jesus. Amen.

"Do not remember the former things,
Nor consider the things of old. Behold,
I will do a new thing,
Now it shall spring forth;
Shall you not know it?
I will even make a road in the wilderness.
And rivers in the desert." Isaiah 43:18-19, NKJV.

A Wilderness Time:

Wilderness times are stages of drought, delaying, and alike feeling lonely.

Times like this can be very isolating, especially when we see God turn out to be silent.

We're doing our best to make it day by day. But we don't feel like we will have a breakthrough.

As we expect the Lord in this period to continue to anoint us into a fresh spirit of joy. Not to get discouraged, or not lose our faith.

Confront the lies of the enemy. Let's use our authority as a believer and servants of God to rebuke the devil's attack.

This time, He tells us to be strong and stand on God's truth. Let's remember wilderness will not be a long journey.

But He is bringing us back to His presence and will come to an end. He has all things in His hands.

Trusting His Words will be a glorious thing to do now. Amen.

Different Seasons:

Going through many different seasons and times of trials and struggles of life. There must be hard battles in spiritual living.

When we have time for our devotion and spending time studying His Word.

It will allow us to build up our daily spiritual strength in the Lord.

Sometimes we don't know what to do to solve our own problems. But when we trust in the name of the Lord Jesus, He never fails us.

"He shall be like a tree,
Planted by the rivers of water,
That brings forth its fruit in its season,
Whose leaf also shall not wither;
And whatever he does shall prosper." Psalm 1:3, NKJV.

I would like to bring up **a few illustrations** of how we go through many seasons of the Christian life.

Seasons of struggles and crises. Seasons of happiness and good health in different times in life.

But we must be confident in the name of the Lord, He is with us and guides our future. Amen.

A Season of Suffering:

As we believe, Jesus suffered for our sins and our sickness. There is no need to suffer for ourselves again.

They crucified Jesus on the cross. He submitted himself with free Will to make a relationship for us.

When He was praying before His crucifixion on the cross, He knew He would suffer for the sins of the world.

He recognized the way the Father is perfect's Will for Him to give Himself up for humankind.

Jesus made a true sacrifice for every mankind in the whole world. Glory to His name. Amen.

"But may the God of all grace, who called us to His eternal glory by Christ Jesus, after *you have suffered a while*, perfect, establish, strengthen, and settle you." 1 Peter 5:10, NKJV.

A Season of Waiting:

There is a time for everything, a time for prayer, and a time for receiving. Many scriptures spoke about waiting upon the Lord.

Waiting is not an interesting solution for some Christians. Waiting on the Lord means; **"hold back," "standing by."**

We're sitting down at the feet of Jesus. Resting in His strength, He will comfort us. We will accept Him to sustain us as we wait on Him.

For some believers, praying can be very challenging, and they are not in a practical situation.

Because when their prayer is finished, they call for an answer right away. Remember what the Lord said to us.

He is bringing all promises to pass; trust in Him and having peace in His presence. Amen.

A Season of Dryness:

Sometimes we go through spiritual dryness. As we don't feel like reading the Word, praying, and even there is no desire to go to the House of God.

Everyone in the Christian faith will go on a journey of dryness. There will be a short season for us, but He takes us back on our right track again.

Because we have received the spirit of God lives in us. He will never leave us alone. He is watching over us and He loves us.

But He is able to strengthen us into His glorious presence. Because of His fresh Word, and His Holy Spirit.

He is giving us His Grace to walk by faith victoriously again. Glory to His name. Amen.

A Season of Preparation:

There is a time to be born-again in the Lord and a time to become mature in spiritual living.

It is a good thing to know what God is preparing us for. We might have some explanations about our destiny as we go through our seasons.

It could be a slow discovery in the spirit realm. But we learn from the Word and grow to build up our spiritual life and receive the strength of the Lord.

It could be a new journey of faith and accepting the Lord Jesus. Taking up our cross to follow Jesus with the right decision to walk by faith.

Living in the Grace and peace of God is a wonderful gift of God. He will prepare us for magnificent opportunities to grow in ministry.

The Holy Spirit leads some into different areas, like, **preaching, teaching, leadership, music, singing, youth, and children's ministry, and more...**

Many Christian believers are trying to use their talents and passion to get prepared to serve in the church.

Some love to serve as prayer warriors, counseling, intercessor. The Lord leads and directs every believer into the right place with the right season.

Although, we all have something to offer our care in the place that the Lord has chosen for us.

We can play a role in all areas and ministry in the body of Christ. He is looking for a passionate heart to be used in His Kingdom.

He wants us to grow and prepare ourselves in the Word to fulfill our call to minister and serve non-believers.

A Season of Rest:

Sometimes, when we're ready to lay down everything on the Alter. He is there and waiting for us that we can sit down in His presence.

He is a wonderful Father who cares for us, and He loves us very much. Having peace in ourselves and walking with the joy of the Lord.

We will stretch out our faith and offer our hearts to rest in God's spirit.

To step up to a stage of maturity and hope for miracles. We must allow ourselves to lay down everything and have peace in the Lord.

God is working in the peaceful atmosphere of His people. If there is chaos and division.

If there is no faith to be found; people cannot understand the miracles of God. He will not perform wonders.

He is the God of peace. He is an awesome God. Also, I believe that non-believers will be interested to discover God's miracles.

God works His wonders to save His people and reveal His glory to us. Amen.

A Seed on the Ground:

God's Word says that when we sow a seed on the ground, we are responsible for the seed.

Let me give an illustration to understand the concept of sowing and reaping.

Let's say we plant a seed of love on the ground because God is love, and we must love others.

Then we give water to the seed because we continue loving and caring. The more we give water by loving God and serving God's people.

Our seeds will grow and grow more to establish a good root. We are expecting a time of harvest and getting ready to reap a good result will be spectacular.

Let me give another example of seed and harvest. We are Christians, and we love Jesus very much.

But in our hearts, we aren't supposed to hate, cheat, lie, and not be jealous.

However, there are a few examples of how we can easily plant seeds on the ground by lack of knowledge.

Even though the Lord is not expecting us to act like non-believers. We are starting to carry with a wrong thought.

We feel it is alright to cheat and to continue doing it by misleading others. In fact, God is observing us.

To be reminded, it is not possible to deceive Him. Knowing in our spirit and our conscience is wrong.

As born-again Christian, we have the Holy Spirit to reveal to us the deceptive activity that is happening.

Anytime we're doing something improper can be against the will of God. He is waiting for us to repent.

We can be sensitive to the seed, which is growing. If we continue to live with a sinful lifestyle, cheating and watering the seed.

Finally, the seed is ready for us to reap the harvest. We reap the harvest with many crises in life.

I would like to point out a few examples of harvest, like:

- *It may be any disaster that would attack by nature.*
- *Having a car accident with severe injury.*
- *Sometimes other people are cheating with an unexpected plan.*

- *Unpredictable, bad sicknesses might attack and would lose a loved one.*
- *It is possible to get complicated by the law.*

There are many examples of reaping a bad harvest after sowing a seed, not to be supposed to plant.

The only way is not to receive a lousy harvest. We need to ask the Lord to remove the seed and the root to be destroyed altogether.

How can we ask the Lord? We ask Him in honesty and humility to repent and remove our sins.

Our God is the God of forgiveness. He can remove every bad seed and replace it with a good harvest for us.

He gives direction on how to plant a good seed on the ground. He loves us, and He cares for all of us. Amen.

A Pruning Time:

In a pruning season, God is testing us in many situations. Because He is equipping us for something bigger.

He sees us there are some characters, ideas, ambitions that need to change.

Sometimes the Lord will warn us to let some people and friends go for a short while.

He is making us ready to meet new people in our next season. It may appear tough and difficult to make a change in every area.

But if we allow Him to develop us to walk in His plan. The Lord is not trying to hurt us. In fact, He is molding and making us good servants of God.

He is serving us to remove our past experiences and old ways of living. Then we will not use these trials and tests in the future.

He prepares us for becoming the men and women of God. He's calling us to grow into loving servants. Amen.

CHAPTER 11

How to become a Christian?

A CHRISTIAN WHO IS a follower of Jesus and trusts in him. The Bible gives a simple explanation so we can have a relationship with Him.

We will have a spiritual experience as we become born-again Christian believers.

The great news of the Christian doctrine appears with the concept that God has chosen us.

He who formed us and created us in the image of His Son on this earth.

I want just to take this opportunity to share how we can have a personal relationship with Jesus by faith.

It is essential to follow the way of God's Word is better than doing any other ritual Christianity. It will not help us to become Christian believers.

Sinned Against God:

When we recognize that we have sinned against God. Our sin will separate us from God, and it will lead us to spiritual death.

We cannot make ourselves clean or forgive our own sins. He came to die on the cross for our iniquities; he sacrificed his life. He shed His blood for our sickness.

Now we can go to Him by faith with no condemnation and no judgment. Becoming a Christian is to have a simple faith in the Lord.

Learning His Word, allowing ourselves to have a fellowship with other Christian believers in the church.

Then we build up our confidence in the Word and live more in the peace of Christ. We grow into a better spiritual maturity in walking with the Lord.

When we move forward in faith, we develop our confidence in the Word of God only. Let's focus on this part that we **"believe"** that Jesus is the Son of God.

We are the sinners; we all need a Savior. He is the One who can save us from our sins. Now we repent our sins and accept Jesus into our hearts.

It is very simple to believe Jesus by faith. I will describe the few steps to remind us to make peace with our Heavenly Father, who loves us.

1. **Believing in One true God and His Word**
2. **Repenting your sins**
3. **Inviting Jesus to come into your heart**
4. **Accepting Jesus as your personal Lord and Savior**
5. **To get baptized in water**
6. **Finding a Christian Fellowship to attend**
7. **Growing in the Spiritual life every day.**

When you follow these simple steps, you become a born-again Christian believer and welcome into God's family.

Forgiven our Sins:

When you are devoting your time in His presence and studying the Word of God, then the Holy Spirit reveals Jesus to you.

I am thrilled that you make the right decision to accept Jesus as your Savior. According to the Bible, you are saved.

He will forgive all your sins and wipe out your tears and restore you from all your iniquities.

Then, remember your name is written in the Book of Life in heaven. I want to lead you a short prayer of salvation.

Repeat after me:

Heavenly Father, I thank you for your Son Jesus; you sent Him to die on the cross for me in my place.

He rose and He is alive again. I repent from all my sins; I invite Jesus to come into my heart;

I believe Jesus is my Lord and my Savior. Thank you for caring for me and accepting me as a child of God. In Jesus' name. Amen.

Conclusion

I WILL CONCLUDE THIS book with the joy of the Lord Jesus. By allowing me to serve you with my spiritual experience.

I am glad I had this opportunity to share my encounter with the Lord. We all desired to know about how we can be able to **'Standing on the Word of God.'**

Creating an exciting topic to be practical for every Christian believer with the help of the Lord.

We will identify that God has been good to His people for guiding them into the right choice.

It was a delight to perform an expression of how we can stand on God's Word.

We must remember the Word of God will never put us down, believing and receiving the correct result.

We need to develop our spiritual knowledge by reading the Word of God.

The more we walk with His Word, love, and wisdom, and we grow more in His understanding.

He desires us to live in wisdom, prosperity, and peace. He wants to renew our faith in a bountiful life.

Jesus encouraged us to seek Him first and spend time in His presence.

This book will help you, motivate you, and prepare you to grow into a mighty man and woman of God.

Every Word can strengthen and inspire you to continue being effective in this life. May this book serve you and refresh you to build up your faith in Christ.

My dream is, this book will reach millions of Christian believers around the world.

Thank you for supporting me, and I am honored to serve you through this book, and may God bless you. Amen.

In the end, I would like to present my other books to you:

- **Parables of Jesus**

- **Healing Miracles of Jesus**
- **Manifestation of Prayer**
- **Authority in the Bible**
- **Preaching with Fire**
- **Encouraging Stories in the Bible**
- **Wisely Decisions in Christ**

About the Author

Dr. Daniel Kazemian has dedicated his life to the nonprofit organization International Evangelistic Ministry, to preach the Good News by the anointing of the Holy Spirit.

In June 1993, he was ordained to the ministry in the National Church of God by Dr. T. L. Lowery in Washington, DC.

He has since become one of today's most dynamic charismatic preachers. Christ walked into his life in January 1985.

Daniel was transformed into an exciting, enthusiastic dynamo for God. He's passionate about sharing God's love and saving grace with everyone, as well as healing the sick.

Daniel started his evangelistic career and his radio/TV ministry in Denmark-Scandinavia and abroad.

He is now serving in the prophetic and healing ministry. He ministers in churches, seminars, conventions, crusades, and anywhere the Spirit of God leads him.

Daniel earned his associate degree from the National Bible College and Seminary in June 1993 in Fort Washington, Maryland.

He received a bachelor's degree, a master's degree, and a Doctor of Theology degree from the International Theological Seminary in July 1996 in Plymouth, Florida.

He is the president of the nonprofit organization, International Evangelistic Ministry, located in Gainesville, Georgia.

Contact him through email:

ieministry@hotmail.com

Visit our website:

www.InternationalEvangelisticMinistry.com